BIRTH OF A SOLO SAILOR

A Voyage between Solitude and Loneliness

by

Maik Ulmschneider

"The strong man is mightiest alone."

Wilhelm Tell I, 3. (Tell)

Friedrich Schiller

www.sailingistruth.com

First edition. Published June 2021

ISBN: 978-3-9823405-0-0 (ebook mobi)

ISBN: 978-3-9823405-1-7 (ebook epub)

ISBN: 978-3-9823405-2-4 (paperback b/w)

ISBN: 978-3-9823405-3-1 (paperback color)

ISBN: 978-3-9823405-4-8 (hardcover premium)

Chart illustration by BMR Williams

Proofread by Johnny Mercer

Cover & layout by Marko Markovic, 5mediadesign

Contents

Choose Your Fate:

Introduction

Dear Reader,

Thank you for keeping me company on my solo passages, in lonely night watches, in endless calms, and in fearful storms. You are there when the enjoyment of solitude turns into loneliness.

Thank you for sharing the beautiful moments with me, too: wild beaches, romantic sunsets, encounters with amazing wildlife. Those moments are so much more enjoyable with you.

Thank you for helping me with the hard work onboard my vessel: down in the sweltering heat of the engine room, up in the dizzy height of the mast or below the boat, cumbersomely cleaning it from growth and barnacles. I don't know where I would take the strength to do this without you.

You keep me company by just reading this book. Turning this page will sign you on to S/V Seefalke for one year. Our route will take us from Suriname in South America to the Yucatán Peninsula in Mexico.

You will see the jungle of Amazonia, the swamps of Florida and tobacco plantations in Cuba. You will meet Haitian freight sailors, Creole jungle kids and Mexican beach gangs. You will encounter whales and turtles and dolphins. And you will see the sea. You will experience it with all its power and beauty.

And as the captain I promise I will not spare you. You will experience the good, the bad and the ugly, and you will get wet. If you want to bail out, now is the time.

Ok, you made your decision. Welcome aboard *Sailing Vessel Seefalke!*

Now you are *Seefalke's* crew, not a virtual crew but a real crew, remote maybe but real, from flesh and blood with heart and soul. And as my crew you will not only join me on my voyage, you will also be involved in the decision making process. Occasionally you will be asked to ***choose your fate*** and take decisions that will change the course of events:

Weather the storm at anchor or better go into a marina? Reef for the night or rather use the breeze to make time?It is up to you. Just remember, we have to bear the consequences together!

Now get moving, you lazy landlubbers and get the ship ready for our first solo passage!

Part One:

On a Mission

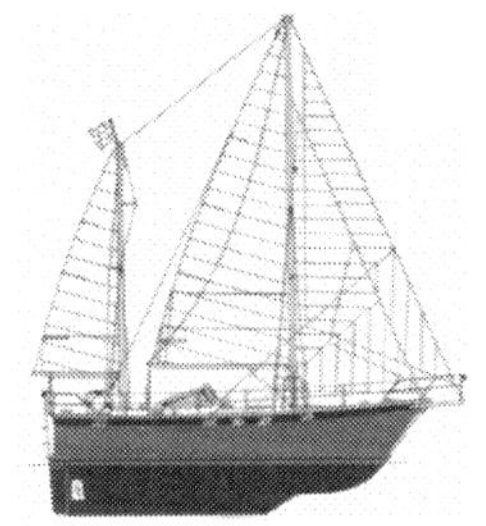

Turning Point Suriname

I have to start this with a confession: Before I planned my route to Paramaribo, the capital of Suriname, I didn't even know where Suriname was. I do not remember if I even knew it existed. If someone would have asked me, I would have put it into Southeast Asia probably or maybe the South Pacific but not into South America. So, don't feel bad if you don't, either.

It is in fact one of the three Guianas, which are, from North to South: Guiana (ex British Guiana), Suriname (ex Dutch Guiana) and French Guiana. Off the beaten path of the milk run route, Suriname is a great stop if you are not afraid of mosquitoes, piranhas, harpies and howling monkeys. If there was not this heat. This relentless, brutal, broiling, sweltering, never-ending equatorial jungle heat that will make your blood boil and your skull burst. The good news, however, Dutch speaking Suriname, that is covered with rain forest by more than eighty percent, is outside the hurricane belt. Its people are welcoming and friendly and its cultural diversity is spectacular, and all this just less than three decades after a bloody civil war.

For me, personally, Suriname marked a dramatic turning point. Whereas up to here, for almost exactly one year, I was traveling together with my American girlfriend and her two Beagles, Cap'n Jack and his sister Scout, it was in the remote jungle that we decided to go separate ways. So, I became a solo sailor by default. Well, at first not entirely, as I still had two canine crew. I had promised to sail them to the first landfall I would make in the United States mainland, 2,500 nautical miles away.

I waited till the last month of the hurricane season and embarked on my first major single-handed voyage: ***Birth of a Solo Sailor.***

Birth of a Solo Sailor

So now it is definite.

It is early morning of October 31st, 2019 as I motor down the muddy waters of Suriname River from Domburg, through the heavy jungle heat. I follow the tide past plantations and mansions towards Paramaribo, Suriname's lively capital, and I know:

It is definite.

S/V Seefalke on Commewijne River in Suriname

Earth and water, just like air and fire, are elements that do not mix well. The relationship broke, the crew was halved. One down, one standing. The math is easy, either way: Two minus one equals one. Two divided by two also equals one. Bottom line is, I am a solo sailor now. Single-handed. I can like it or not, it is what it is.

Approaching Jules Wijdenbosh Bridge

I am approaching the visually impressive 164 ft high and 4,934 ft long Jules Wijdenbosh Bridge, or "Bosje Bridge" as the locals call it. It reminds me of the new Rügendamm Bridge that connects Rügen, Germany's largest island, with the mainland. I had a clear view on it from my slip in my homeport. I remember the Baltic Sea where I did a lot of solo sailing. I remember how every single weekend it was a welcome escape from my office life. The boat was my hideaway. Sometimes my kids or my wife would join me but the vast majority of the time, it was just me. I remember how I loved it. The solitude. The tranquility. How I gained strength from it for my life back in society.

My homeport is the picturesque and historic Hanseatic city of Stralsund. From here I ventured out to eastern German islands like Rügen or Hiddensee. I also loved to sail to Poland and Denmark. The Danish island Bornholm, 80 nautical miles from Stralsund was always a challenge because it mostly involved an over-night passage. Sometimes I made it up to Karlskrona in Sweden and through the archipelago off the Swedish coast all the way to Kalmar or even Stockholm. Back in the day, that was my backyard, my home turf.

Now, since I crossed the Atlantic and sailed waters way more challenging than the Baltic Sea, that in the big scheme is nothing else than a glacier puddle, something in my head pictures the Baltic Sea as a children's playground which of course, is a huge misconception. Make no mistake, the Baltic Sea is as dangerous as any sea with an uncounted number of wrecks on its bottom proving the point.

But 80 nautical miles to Bornholm, a challenge?? The passage I am just starting will be around 700 nautical miles and I would not even consider *that* long. A trip as short as 700 nautical miles would not even make it to my personal top five anymore, barely to my top ten. But it will lead me through waters I have never sailed before. Increasing the stakes, I will do it all by myself. No helping hand will be there and no company, nobody to share the sunsets with, nobody to blame if things go wrong, nobody to lean on to if things turn tough. But on the bright side, there won't be talking when I need quietude, no presence when I need solitude, no complaining when I need fortitude.

I feel light, maybe even a bit light-headed, relieved of the burden of responsibility. And as I am wedging in between the mighty pillars of Bosje Bridge and trying to decide if I take the starboard or port channel around the half-sunken wreck of the Goslar, I get distracted by bits and pieces of her history:

The German motor vessel Goslar got surprised by the outbreak of WWII and was seeking neutral territory in Dutch Guiana (today Suriname). Camouflaged, flying a pretend US flag, she dropped anchor in Suriname River in September 1939. When the German Wehrmacht invaded the Netherlands on May 10th, 1940 an order was given to detain every German citizen of the age of 15 and older. Before they got arrested, the dutiful crew sank their ship in the Suriname River where she still lies today, dividing the shipping lane as a silent witness of those peace-less days.

The wreck of the German motor vessel Goslar in Suriname River

I take the channel to my port side because i t will bring me closer to the city. I crave to feel the vibes one last time and catch one last glance at the city that was my home for the last four months. As I pass the HQ of the Maritime Authority of Suriname (MAS) I check out on VHF as formally required. The bored voice of the MAS radio operator tells me, he cannot figure why it is actually required, either. It will take another four hours to reach the open ocean, but I already feel free. Free of responsibilities and free of obligations.

Last sight of Paramaribo

I head out of the mighty river mouth; dolphins are welcoming me to the ocean. Dolphins, aren't they the ultimate symbols of freedom and independence? But then I think, they live in pods, they have company, protection and hierarchy. Not quite my definition of independence.

This makes me want to hear that great song of the German bard Reinhard Mey, 'Einhandsegler' (Solo Sailor). Damn it! I didn't download it and cell service is already gone.

So, I start singing it to myself: 'Nobody stands by you, nobody stands above you... hmm hmmm hm (I don't remember all the lyrics.) You are nobody's subject, and nobody is subject to you.' Yep, this is how it is, and how I love it!

Free of obligations is actually not quite true. I had promised friends and family of the crew of the *Bourbon Rhode* to take a little detour and watch out for any signs of life for the seven crew still missing. The164 ft offshore tug *Bourbon Rhode* sank in hurricane Lorenzo four weeks ago, on September 26th, 2019 after failure of her azimuth thrusters on her way from the Canaries to Guiana. Azimuth thrusters are great for precise manoeuvring but if they fail during a storm, the ship is doomed, losing propulsion and steering at the same time.

Three crew members were rescued, four were recovered dead, but till now, two life rafts and seven crew members have not been accounted for and hope dies last. The official rescue operation was ceased after which friends and family of the missing crew members started unparalleled efforts to reach out to sailors in the area to help find their loved ones.

Offshore tugboat Bourbon Rhode[1]

1 Usually I only use original images in this book. For this story, however, I decided to use these two images of the Bourbon Rhode and her missing crew to try to visualize the personal dimension of this tragedy. It is not just an anonymous news item, but real people who have families and friends grieving for them. Credits: File image courtesy Bourbon Offshore

Dino Miškić

Andrii Izmailskyi

Edwin Furog

Viacheslav Kovalchuk

Dmytro Kozyrev

Oleksandr Korshykov

Yevgenii Melgunov

Oleg Kravets

Missing crew of the Bourbon Rhode[2]

2 Credits to Bourbon Rhode Rescue Facebook Group

Well aware that the chances are marginal in the vast endlessness of the Atlantic Ocean, assisting the search effort is a natural thing to do. Those men are family to me as much as they are to their own relatives. There is this invisible band that ties all sailors together. I know they would have done the same for me. So even we solo sailors are never alone, really.

So, when I leave Suriname waters, I tack out a good bit to the North before I go on my charted course to Martinique. It is a beam reach course and the wind is fierce, a steady force 6. I sail under my boomed jib and second reef in the main. The seas are building up, *Seefalke* is rocking and rolling, but steadily I am bringing more and more distance between the land memories and my current state of mind.

Grey in grey during the day, black in black during the night, I don't see a single soul. Neither dead nor alive, neither human nor animal. Almost impossible to spot a life raft, drifting in the boiling seas. Those poor guys! When I leave the forecasted drifting area of the *Bourbon Rhode* life rafts behind me, my heart and my thoughts are with those brave men who went to sea and will never see home again.

If they could go down, experienced seamen on a huge ship, why wouldn't I on my tiny tin can?

I remember that famous quote. I think it was Aristotle who first said it, but I could be wrong: 'There are three kinds of men: the living, the dead and those at sea.' I start to understand what he meant. While you are at sea, especially when you are just by yourself, you are as far from the dead as you are from the living. An act of the gods of the seas may easily push you to the one or the other edge. It sounds frightening at first, but when I start to deeply, really understand the full meaning, it makes me unbelievably relaxed.

When I met solo sailors in the past, I always thought they were a bit weird to say the least. Marcel, for instance, the retired lawyer from the South of France, who could never convince his wife to join him sailing but was never short of female company at anchorages or in marinas. I barely ever saw him wearing clothes.

Or Paul from Belgium, the most peaceful person I ever met, who would take even the worst news with a smile. I thought he constantly was high as a kite. Now I understand that they already arrived where I am still heading: complete inner peace. They have reached their comfort zone right in-between the living and the dead. What would ever worry them there?

Not quite there yet, I still get a little worried when an evil squall will not let me out of its claws, and I spend almost an entire day going in circles. Frustrated. Tired. Exhausted. Still 200 nautical miles to Barbados. When the weather clears, I finally fall asleep dead tired. In sheer disbelief I realize I must have passed out for hours when I make my new logbook entry.

All of a sudden, it is good I am still far out, otherwise it could have brought me closer to the dead than I am ready for yet. As I am approaching Barbados, I come so close to the island that I can smell the barbecues on the beaches of Bridgetown. It takes all my strength of will to overcome my desire to seek shelter and comfort there but keep on sailing.

Once the lights of Barbados are sinking behind the horizon, I feel stronger and more powerful than ever. I have won over myself. I am conqueror of the seven seas, king of the world! At the heights of my superiority inebriety I feel like Wilhelm Tell in Friedrich Schiller's epic drama.

"The strong man is mightiest alone," is what he said.

If I would have known back in high school, when they made us read all these ancient door-stoppers, that one day the literary prose would give me encouragement and strength in lonely and fearful night watches while out in the middle of the ocean, I would sure have remembered more of it than just this single line.

As the night seems to drag on to eternity and the inebriety yields to a fully-grown emotional hangover, my thoughts drift onto the old Prussian virtues: courage and discipline of course, those are the easy ones. Fortitude without self-pity, conscientiousness and toughness, which translates to 'Be hard on yourself and learn to suffer without complaining!' I feel how I instinctively tension my chin muscles just thinking about them, the little Prussian share of blood in my veins flows a little faster. Finally, the moon rises and breaks the impervious blackness of the night and my mind.

"Hell", I think, "the old Prussians would be proud of me!" I smile.

And with a smile everything is easier. Paul from Belgium knew that already.

The remaining 100 nautical miles to Martinique are kindergarten. As I drop the anchor in Sainte-Anne, I am almost disappointed this challenging passage is already over. While I have reached the destination of this passage, I realize I am still just at the beginning of the epic voyage to know myself.

And this is what solo sailing is all about.

From Martinique to Puerto Rico

Dropping anchor in the crystal-clear turquoise water of the Caribbean after months that I only saw muddy river water was a magical moment. For the first time I missed someone to share it with. At sea I enjoy the solitude, it is after arrival at the destinations that I miss company. The dogs are great. Over the last week's passage I developed a very special, indeed intimate relationship with them. We shared our bunks, the weather, our watches and our food, yes, we even shared our plates. They never complained.

We did not stay in Martinique for long and this was also our only stop there, because for some reason I thought I was in a hurry to take Cap'n Jack and Scout home. It was only after I arrived in Les Saintes, that small archipelago south of Guadeloupe, that I decided to make this delivery an adventure on its own and actually enjoy it. When I left Sainte-Anne on Martinique I was torn. Torn between my promise to deliver the dogs as fast as possible to the United States and the temptation to spend more time in this intriguingly beautiful part of the world. Should I stop in Dominica or not? Should I maybe even make more stops in Martinique? Or should I rush to Puerto Rico in a non-stop passage? I decided to go for a compromise and sail to the legendary pirate haven Iles de Saintes. So, I headed north making use of the trade winds. I remember this was a stop-and-go passage.

The wind in these latitudes is constant, strongly blowing from the northeast. When I was in the lee of those 5,000 ft high volcanoes of the Lesser Antilles I had trouble catching any. I could have taken a route further offshore but I was targeting the cell service of these islands. Then, all of a sudden, when I got between the islands, the funnel effect would accelerate the wind to near-gale force within minutes. Stop and go.

During this stop-and-go passage, the entire afternoon of November 8th, 2019, I was looking forward to the sunset. The skies were meticulously clear with an exception of just the powerful clouds piling up around the mighty volcanoes. While I was getting my gear ready for what I thought would become a stunning sunset, one of those squalls suddenly made it over the mountains and pressed on the lee side of the island, ruthlessly depriving me of my sunset.

Deprived of the sunset

I arrived at Iles des Saintes in torrential rain feeling like a pirate threading between high mountains through Passe du Pain de Sucre, the Sugar-bread Pass, into the well protected bay of Anse Mire where I caught a mooring buoy. I remember Iles des Saint had two faces: One was when the big cruise ships arrived and the islands, especially the main island, Terre-de-Haut, were flooded by tourists, the other was when they were gone and the island turned into a forgotten paradise again. I usually stayed on my boat when the cruise ships anchored in the bay because this was also when the prices went up.

After one week I set sail again heading for Culebra, a beautiful small island east of Puerto Rico, where I checked in to the United States and obtained my cruising permit. This place was recommended to me in a Facebook sailing group and I would not be disappointed. I spent ten days in this interesting place, it was so much different from the Lesser Antilles, much drier and rockier but still with amazing wild beaches. It would become one of my favourite spots in the Caribbean.

Hector El Protector in Culebra

Here I waited for my son Tom to join me for his Thanksgiving holidays. Tom goes to college in Mobile, Alabama. He flew into San Juan in Puerto Rico, where we met and set sail together for our next destination: Samana in the Dominican Republic.

This was when I learned an expensive lesson. You know, there are these $1,000 nights. $1,000 nights are notorious among sailors. This is what we call nights when a sail is ripped in a sudden gust, or the dinghy outboard motor falls overboard, or the anchor needs to be given up. Ask any blue-water sailor and you will find they all had at least one of those $1,000 nights in their careers, even though they might not like being reminded of it. Most of the time it is not the night that causes the loss, as the term may imply, but sheer skipper's negligence, leaving an ugly stain on the captain's record.

So now you know how hard it is for me to talk about it. But it has been a while, so I am kind of over it and ready to make my confession. The following story is one of the two ***Choose-Your-Fate*** stories in this book. This is where you can decide if you are a crew member or a passenger. If you want to just lay back and enjoy the ride, please jump to "Hit by a $3,000 Gust - Original" (page *49*). If you want to be part of the crew and ***choose your fate***, just continue reading.

Choose Your Fate:

Hit by a $3,000 Gust

0

My son Tom joined me in San Juan, Puerto Rico, USA for a week of sailing and some land exploration. He has often sailed with me and is quite experienced for his young age of 17, but he has never sailed in tropical waters before.

The sun shines bright as we weigh anchor and head through the narrow channel of San Juan harbor out into the open sea, passing gigantic docks, huge cruise ships, the impressive Coast Guard base, the vast oil terminal and finally, the proud San Felippe del Morro Castle. Now nothing but the horizon separates us from our destination. A light breeze pushes us forward gently, riply wavelets are burbling along our bright orange hull, glittering in the Caribbean sun.

Relaxed sailing: humans

Relaxed sailing: canines

Our destination is Marina Puerto Bahia on the Samana peninsula in the Dominican Republic. A short 200 nm sail – just two days and two nights. As we leave the channel, we turn port to WNW on a half-wind course, heading straight for Samana. A perfect sailing day, relaxed and quiet. It's so relaxed and quiet that Tom falls asleep on the foredeck, my boat dogs Cap'n Jack and Scout snooze in the cockpit, snuggled up tightly, and I am drifting away listening to my favorite audiobook. Only the auto-pilot is doing its work untiringly, keeping us on course as if we are gliding on magic rails.

When Tom wakes up later and I make some dinner, he is a little disappointed about the meager mileage covered and our current speed that barely exceeds three knots. But the sunset is beautiful and well rested as he is, he agrees to take the first night watch while I nestle down in my bunk without the slightest premonition of the price tag this negligence might have.

As usual, I fall asleep fast. We solo sailors are able to sleep wherever and whenever we have the opportunity because they are rare. But as always a part of me stays awake, subconsciously listening to the sound of the wind and the waves and sensing the boat‘s movements. I feel a breeze on my face. I like it. It is hot in the cabin and the breeze feels good!

But a breeze? A BREEZE? Argh, this means I forgot to close the hatches! I must have forgotten to close them before we weighed anchor. Damnit!!!

Are you getting up to close the hatches? In this case continue reading on page 25 (section 1.1)

Or will you do it later when you get up for your watch? In this case continue reading on page 27 section 1.2)

Choose Your Fate:

Hit by a $3,000 Gust

1.1

You decided to close the hatches before you go to sleep.

I feel a breeze on my face. I like it. It is hot in the cabin and the breeze feels good!

But a breeze? A BREEZE? Argh, this means I forgot to close the hatches! I must have forgotten to close them before we weighed anchor. Damnit! I am way too lazy to get up. But if I don't close them and we get hit by one of those evil squalls we'll make tons of water. So, hesitantly and swearing like a trooper, I get up again and close the hatches without a clue as to how much money I just saved.

Then I crawl back into my bunk, cuddle up with Cap'n Jack and get ready for my well-deserved nap. But then I remember that we are still sailing under full sails. Normally I reef at sunset. Because you cannot see those squalls at night and the gusts will be over you before you have time to shout "Reef!". I do that even when the winds are light and I would love to make time. But I learned it the hard way that it is better to lose a day than to lose a sail. Or more.

But I am so damn tired! If I reef the sails now, I may as well stay up.

Are you getting up again to reef the sails? In this case continue reading on page 29 (section 1.1.1)

Are you too tired and decide to stay in bed? In this case continue reading on page 33 (section 1.1.2)

Choose Your Fate:

Hit by a $3,000 Gust

1.2

You decided to wait to close the hatches till you get up for your watch.

I feel a breeze on my face. I like it. It is hot in the cabin and the breeze feels good!

But a breeze? A BREEZE? Argh, this means I forgot to close the hatches! I must have forgotten to close them before we weighed anchor. Damnit!! But I am way too lazy to get up, so I just enjoy the breeze and keep sleeping. I will close them when I get up for my watch.

But then I remember that we are still sailing under full sails. Normally I reef at sunset. Because you cannot see those squalls at night and the gusts will be over you before you have time to spell "reef". I do that even when the winds are light and I would love to make time. But I learned it the hard way that it is better to lose a day than to lose a sail. Or more.

But I am so damned tired! If I reef the sails now, I may as well stay up.

Are you getting up again to reef the sails? In this case continue reading on page 39 (section 1.2.1)

Are you too tired and decide to stay in bed? In this case continue on page 43 (reading section 1.2.2)

Choose Your Fate:

Hit by a $3,000 Gust

1.1.1

You decided to get up again and reef the sails for the night.

Then I crawl back into my bunk, cuddle up with Cap'n Jack and get ready for my well deserved nap. But then I remember that we are still sailing under full sails. Normally I reef at sunset. Because you cannot see those squalls at night and the gusts will be over you before you have time to spell "reef". I do that even if the winds are light and I would love to make time. But I learned it the hard way that it is better to lose a day than to lose a sail. Or more.

I am so damned tired! If I reef the sails now, I can as well stay up. But I have to do it. I remember once, when we were knocked flat on the water by one of those evil gusts that came out of nowhere. If this happens now with Tom at the helm, he could easily get catapulted out of the cockpit and go overboard with consequences I don't even want to imagine.

So I get up, again, and Tom helps me to reef the mainsail and take down the mizzen. I decide to keep the genoa at full size. It is quickly furled away in case a squall hits. Tom is very disappointed because, after we are finished with our reefing maneuver our log shows just two knots. We just lost one very valuable knot. But safety first. I try another attempt and return to my bunk where Cap'n Jack and Scout are already waiting for me. Finally, and relieved that I did what I had to do, I fall asleep momentarily.

"Five knots, five and a half!," Tom's excited voice breaks my sweet dreams.

We are heeling a little and the well audible whooshing confirms his announcements.

"Six, six and a half!"

For a moment I feel like I am on board the German WWII submarine *U96* in the movie "The Boat", when they keep falling after they got hit by a depth charge in the Straits of Gibraltar. Tom's speed reports sound just like the submarine's chief engineer's diving depth reports that end with "I report obediently: Boat is uncontrollable."

"BOAT IS UNCONTROLLABLE!," it echoes in my head, exactly in the moment when Tom cheers "Seven knots, yieeeha!"

7.5 knots is *Seefalke's* hull speed if I remember it correctly. She is not supposed to go faster than seven knots. She is not DESIGNED to go faster than seven knots through the water! The heeling has gotten to an impressive thirty degree tilt. I have trouble jumping out of my bunk.

Through the unbearable noise of the howling wind I scream: "Tom, slack the sheets!"

Tom cannot hear me, the noise of the wind and the waves are just too loud. When I finally make it into the cockpit I see Tom with a happy grin chasing this poor boat through the breaking seas. The boiling sea is black with green and red froth reflecting the spooky shine of the navlights. I take over the helm, take some pressure off the sheets and furl away the genoa, replacing it with my cutter jib. And so we continue with a good speed of 6.5 knots.

Nightfall

I make my logbook entry: 2400hrs: Wind NE to ENE force 6 gusting 9, seas 7 ft increasing 10 ft, heavy rain, genoa reefed away, set jib proceeding under main 1st reef and jib, HDG 295, COG 285, SOG 4.2 kts. Maik on watch.

When I make the midnight entry into the logbook I see Tom is still sitting there, motionless, pale, with empty eyes. I understand how he feels. I hug him and I apologize. I apologize for not briefing him properly about the perniciousness of tropical squalls.

If you want to see what happened in reality, go to page 49 and read "Hit by a $3,000 Gust - Original"

Choose Your Fate:

Hit by a $3,000 Gust

1.1.2

You decided to stay in bed and not reef the sails.

Then I crawl back into my bunk, cuddle up with Cap'n Jack and get ready for my well deserved nap. But then I remember that we are still sailing under full sails. Normally I reef at sunset. Because you cannot see those squalls at night and the gusts will be over you before you have time to shout "Reef!". I do that even if the winds are light and I would love to make time. But I learned the hard way that it is better to lose a day than to lose a sail. Or more.

But I am so damned tired! If I reef the sails now, I can as well stay up. I try to remember the weather forecast. I cannot remember it said anything about squalls. The skies didn't look like there would be too much squall activity in the night, either. And so, contemplating the weather forecast and the skies I drift into my dreams.

"Five knots, five and a half!," Tom's excited voice breaks my sweet dreams.

We are heeling a little and the well audible whooshing confirms his announcements.

"Six, six and a half!." For a moment I feel like I am on board the German WWII submarine *U96* in the movie "The Boat", when they keep falling after they got hit by a depth charge in the Straits of Gibraltar. Tom's speed reports sound just like the submarine's chief engineer's diving depth reports that end with "I report obediently: Boat is uncontrollable."

"BOAT IS UNCONTROLLABLE!," it echoes in my head, exactly in the moment when Tom cheers "Seven knots, yieeeha!"

7.5 knots is *Seefalke's* hull speed if I remember it correctly. She is not supposed to go faster than seven knots. She is not DESIGNED to go faster than seven knots through the water! The heeling has gotten to an unhealthy thirty degree tilt, maybe more. I have trouble jumping out of my bunk.

Through the unbearable noise of the howling wind I scream "Tom, slack the sheets!"

When I finally stand on my feet with one on the wall and one on the bunk, tightly grasping the ceiling handrail while desperately trying to gain enough stability to move out of the cabin and into the cockpit, it knocks me over and off my feet completely. The wall becomes the floor, the aisle becomes the new wall. I am so glad, I closed those hatches. No guessing how much water would have made it into the cabin now as the portholes are completely submerged. Somehow, bruised and soaked from sweat and I don't remember how, I make it into the cockpit, desperately hoping Tom is still there.

And yes, he is, standing on the cockpit's side wall grasping the steering wheel in despair. Finally, after what seems like an eternity but can't have been more than a few seconds, I reach the cleats and tear loose the sheets, main first then genoa. Immediatel y the boat comes upright and the sound of the shivering sails becomes unbearable. I need to take the genoa down or it will tear like toilet paper. The boiling sea is black with green and red froth reflecting the spooky shine of the nav lights.

Nightfall

With nothing on but my underpants, no time to put on a life vest or a PLB (Personal Life Beacon), I carefully crawl forward on all fours to the foredeck, sliding wildly with Seefalke performing her worst rodeo. I hear myself talking to her to calm her down. Uncounted bangs and bruises later I make it to the halyard. It takes some effort and some risky maneuvering to tame and take down this large fabric, I eventually get it done, but not before the large shackle at the sail tack lands a good swing on my face leaving me with a split lip, a tooth less and a mouthful of blood. It hurts badly yet there is no time for pity right now. It could have been worse and hit me in the eye, for example. So I spit out the tooth and swallow the blood. Or was it the other way around? I don't know.

When I turn around to crawl back aft, I get hit by more spume smacking over the sea fence. Blood, sweat and tears are running down my face, and instinctively I think of Churchill and his historic speech. Still giggling with amusement and the beginnings of madness, I slide back into the safe and dry cockpit and haul in the main sheet, finally regaining control over this vessel.

"Holy Moly," I think, "that was a close call!"

And I sit down and try to relax holding my swollen and bloody mouth. Cap'n Jack peers up to me as if he wanted to ask if it is safe now. So I nod down the companionway, his signal that it is ok to come up. But where is the other one? Where is Scout?

I can't see her in the main cabin where she was snuggled up to me under my blanket sleeping before the hell broke loose. I feel panic coming up. If she had gone overboard during the knockdown she is history. No way to find her pitch black body in the pitch black night in the pitch black water. No chance! Not the slightest. Anything else is sheer delusion. But hope dies last so I go down into the main cabin. I hadn't seen her coming up earlier, but really I don't know. Maybe she just hid somewhere, crawled deeper under the blanket or underneath the bunk or into the stern cabin. As I step down the rear companionway into the stern cabin I see the reflection of her eyes in the very stern, snuggled up to the spare sails and lines. Relief!

As I come closer with my flashlight I see the cushion underneath her is wet. No blood, no sweat and also no tears, but it is ok. The accident is just fine! She is fine! Good girl! I take her in my arms and hold her tiny shivering body tight as we slowly move back into the cockpit where Cap'n Jack welcomes her back to life.

Logbook entry 2400hrs: *"Wind NE to ENE force 6 gusting 9, seas 7 ft increasing 10 ft, heavy rain, got knocked down in squall line, boat ok, crew ok, no visible damages, genoa reefed away, proceeding under mainsail only, HDG 295, COG 285, SOG 4.2 kts. Maik on watch."*

When I make the midnight entry into the logbook I see Tom is still sitting there, motionless, pale, with empty eyes. I understand how he feels. He thinks it was his fault that I lost a tooth, I almost went overboard, we almost lost a dog and we almost capsized, because he hauled in the sheets rather than slack them during the fierce gusts. But it isn't. Not at all. It was all my fault.

I hug him and I apologize. I apologize for not briefing him properly about the perniciousness of tropical squalls. I apologize for not reefing at sunset as I usually do. Two absolutely inexcusable mistakes that almost cost a ship, two human and two canine lives.

If you want to see what happened in reality, go to page 49 and read "Hit by a $3,000 Gust - Original"

Choose Your Fate:

Hit by a $3,000 Gust

1.2.1

You decided to get up again and reef the sails for the night

But then I remember that we are still sailing under full sails. Normally I reef at sunset, because you cannot see those squalls at night and the gusts will be over you before you have time to spell "reef". I do that even if the winds are light and I would love to make time. But I learned it the hard way that it is better to lose a day than to lose a sail. Or more. But I am so damned tired! If I reef the sails now, I may as well stay up.

But I have to do it. I remember once, when we were put flat on the water by one of those evil gusts that came out of nowhere. If this happens now with Tom at the helm, he could easily get catapulted out of the cockpit and go overboard with consequences I don't even want to imagine. So I get up, again, and Tom helps me to reef the mainsail and take down the mizzen. I decide to keep the genoa at full size. It is quickly furled away in case a squall hits. Tom is very disappointed because, after we are finished with our reefing maneuver our log shows just two knots. We just lost one very valuable knot. But safety first. I try another attempt and return to my bunk where Cap'n Jack and Scout are already waiting for me. Finally, and relieved that I did what I had to do, I fall asleep momentarily.

“Five knots, five and a half!,” Tom‘s excited voice breaks my sweet dreams.

We are heeling a little and the well audible whooshing confirms his announcements.

“Six, six and a half!.“ For a moment I feel like I am on board the German WWII submarine *U96* in the movie “The Boat“, when they keep falling after they got hit by a depth charge in the Straits of Gibraltar. Tom‘s speed reports sound just like the submarine‘s chief engineer‘s diving depth reports that end with “I report obediently: Boat is uncontrollable.“

“BOAT IS UNCONTROLLABLE!,“ it echoes in my head, exactly in the moment when Tom cheers “Seven knots, yieeeha!“

7.5 knots is *Seefalke*‘s hull speed if I remember it correctly. She is not supposed to go faster than seven knots. She is not DESIGNED to go faster than seven knots through the water! The heeling has gotten to an impressive 30 degree tilt. I have trouble jumping out of my bunk.

Through the unbearable noise of the howling wind I scream: “Tom, slack the sheets!”

Tom cannot hear me, the noise of the wind and the waves are just too loud. All of a sudden water is hitting me in the face, shooting through the open hatches so brutally and vehemently I have the feeling it pushes my eyes deep into my skull. I lose sight, the noise is deafening and I can hardly breathe. I get a little glimpse of how it must be to drown. Not peaceful at all!! I spit salty water. Somehow, and I don’t remember how, I make it into the cockpit, desperately hoping Tom is still there. The boiling sea is black with green and red froth reflecting the spooky shine of the nav lights. I take over the helm, take some pressure off the sheets and furl away the genoa, replacing it with my cutter jib. And so we continue with a good speed of 6.5 knots.

Nightfall

I make my logbook entry: *"2400hrs: Wind NE to ENE force 6 gusting 9, seas 7 ft increasing 10 ft, heavy rain, genoa reefed away, set jib, proceeding under main 1st reef and jib, HDG 295, COG 285, SOG 4.2 kts. Maik on watch."*

When I make the midnight entry into the logbook I see Tom is still sitting there, motionless, pale, with empty eyes. I understand how he feels. I hug him and I apologize. I apologize for not briefing him properly about the perniciousness of tropical squalls. On the other hand I am happy that I still got up to reef the sails. No guessing what could have happened with all sails up.

This is what I recall as I stand in the Apple service shop in Leipzig, Germany when the young computer specialist breaks the news to me that my MacBook Pro (newest generation) is a total write-off. In fact, it's beyond that. Neither him nor anyone else in the shop had ever seen anything like it. The laptop was in its case during the incident but a few drops of salt water made it inside. It still looks new from the outside but inside there is not a single component left that is not completely corroded or salt frozen. He says the repair would be 4,000 EUR but a new one would only be 2,000 EUR.

I think of the five lives that we didn't lose that night, and I think to myself, all in all, I got a good deal here. In fact, that $3,000 gust seems like quite a bargain...

So I take a photo of the wreck for my story and leave the store with a smile.

Squall casualty

If you want to see what happened in reality, go to page 49 and read "Hit by a $3,000 Gust - Original"

Choose Your Fate:

Hit by a $3,000 Gust

1.2.2

You decided to stay in bed and not reef the sails.

But then I remember that we are still sailing under full sails. Normally I reef at sunset. Because you cannot see those squalls at night and the gusts will be over you before you have time to shout "Reef!". I do that even if the winds are light and I would love to make time. But I learned it the hard way that it is better to lose a day than to lose a sail. Or more. But I am so damned tired! If I reef the sails now, I can as well stay up. I try to remember the weather forecast. I cannot remember it said anything about squalls. The skies didn't look like there would be too much squall activity in the night, either. And so, contemplating the weather forecast and the skies I drift into my dreams.

"Five knots, five and a half!," Tom's excited voice breaks my sweet dreams.

We are heeling a little and the well audible whooshing confirms his announcements.

"Six, six and a half!." For a moment I feel like I am on board the German WWII submarine *U96* in the movie "The Boat", when they keep falling after they got hit by a depth charge in the Straits of Gibraltar. Tom's speed reports sound just like the submarine's chief engineer's diving depth reports that end with "I report obediently: Boat is uncontrollable."

"BOAT IS UNCONTROLLABLE!," it echoes in my head, exactly in the moment when Tom cheers "Seven knots, yieeeha!"

7.5 knots is *Seefalke's* hull speed if I remember it correctly. She is not supposed to go faster than seven knots. She is not DESIGNED to go faster than seven knots through the water! The heeling has gotten to an unhealthy 30 degree tilt, maybe more. I have trouble jumping out of my bunk.

Through the unbearable noise of the howling wind I scream "Tom, slack the sheets!"

When I finally stand on my feet with one on the wall and one on the bunk, tightly grasping the ceiling handrail while desperately trying to gain enough stability to move out of the cabin and into the cockpit, it knocks me over and off my feet completely. The wall becomes the floor, the aisle becomes the new wall as water is hitting me in the face, shooting through the open hatches so brutally and vehemently I have the feeling it pushes my eyes deep into my skull. I lose sight, the noise is deafening and I can hardly breathe. I get a little glimpse of how it must be to drown. Not peaceful at all!! I spit salty water. Somehow, and I don't remember how, I make it into the cockpit, desperately hoping Tom is still there.

And yes, he is, standing on the cockpit's sidewalls grasping to the steering wheel in despair. Finally, after what seems like an eternity but can't have been more than a few seconds, I reach the cleats and tear loose the sheets, main first then genoa. Immediately the boat comes upright and the sound of the shivering sails becomes unbearable. I need to take the genoa down or it will tear like toilet paper. The boiling sea is black with green and red froth reflecting the spooky shine of the nav lights.

Nightfall

With nothing on but my underpants, no time to put on a life vest or a PLB (Personal Life Beacon), I carefully crawl forward on all fours to the foredeck, sliding wildly with Seefalke performing her worst rodeo. I hear myself talking to her to calm her down. Uncounted bangs and bruises later I make it to the halyard. It takes some effort and some risky maneuvering to tame and take down this large fabric, but eventually I get it done. But not before the large shackle at the sail tack lands a good swing on my face leaving me with a split lip, a tooth less and a mouthful of blood. It hurts badly but there is no time for pity right now. It could have been worse and hit me in the eye, for example. So I spit out the tooth and swallow the blood. Or was it the other way around? I don't know.

When I turn around to crawl back aft, I get hit by more spume smacking over the sea fence. Blood, sweat and tears are running down my face, and instinctively I think of Churchill and his historic speech. Still giggling of amusement and beginning madness, I slide back into the safe and dry cockpit and haul in the main sheet, finally regaining control over this vessel.

"Holy Moly," I think, "that was a close call!"

And I sit down and try to relax holding my swollen and bloody mouth. Cap'n Jack peers up to me as if he wanted to ask if it is safe now. So I nod down the companionway, his signal that it is ok to come up. But where is the other one? Where is Scout? I can't see her in the main cabin where she was snuggled up to me under my blanket sleeping before the hell broke loose. I feel panic coming up. If she had gone overboard during the knockdown she is history. No way to find her pitch black body in the pitch black night in the pitch black water. No chance! Not the slightest. Anything else is sheer delusion. But hope dies last so I go down into the main cabin. I hadn't seen her coming up earlier, but really I don't know. Maybe she just hid somewhere, crawled deeper under the blanket or underneath the bunk or into the stern cabin. As I step down the rear companionway into the stern cabin I see the reflection of her eyes in the very stern, snuggled up to the spare sails and lines. Relief! As I come closer with my flashlight I see the cushion underneath her is wet. No blood, no sweat and also no tears, but it is ok. The accident is just fine! She is fine! Good girl! I take her in my arms and hold her tiny shivering body tight as we slowly move back into the cockpit where Cap'n Jack welcomes her back to life.

Logbook entry 2400hrs: *"Wind NE to ENE force 6 gusting 9, seas 7 ft increasing 10 ft, heavy rain, got knocked down in squall line, boat ok, crew ok, no visible damages, genoa reefed away, proceeding under mainsail only, HDG 295, COG 285, SOG 4.2 kts. Maik on watch."*

When I make the midnight entry into the logbook I see Tom is still sitting there, motionless, pale, with empty eyes. I understand how he feels. He thinks it was his fault that I lost a tooth, I almost went overboard, we almost lost a dog and we almost capsized, because he hauled in the sheets rather than slack them during the fierce gusts. But it isn't. Not at all. It was all my fault.

I hug him and I apologize. I apologize for not briefing him properly about the perniciousness of tropical squalls. I apologize for not reefing at sunset as I usually do. I apologize that I didn't shut the hatches when we weighed the anchor. Three absolutely inexcusable mistakes that almost cost a ship, two human and two canine lives.

This is what I recall as I stand in the Apple service shop in Leipzig, Germany when the young computer specialist breaks the news to me that my MacBook Pro (newest generation) is a total write-off. In fact, it's beyond that. Neither him nor anyone else in the shop had ever seen anything like it. The laptop was in its case during the incident but a few drops of salt water made it inside. It still looks new from the outside but inside there is not a single component left that is not completely corroded or salt frozen. He says the repair would be 4,000 EUR but a new one would only be 2,000 EUR.

I think of the five lives that we didn't lose that night, and I think to myself, all in all, I got a good deal here. In fact, that 3,000 USD gust seems like quite a bargain...

So I take a photo of the wreck for my story and leave the store with a smile.

Squall casualty

Hit by a $3,000 Gust - ORIGINAL

My son Tom joined me in San Juan, Puerto Rico, USA for a week of sailing and some land exploration. He has often sailed with me and is quite experienced for his age of 17, but he has never sailed in tropical waters before. The sun shines bright as we weigh anchor and head through the narrow channel of San Juan harbor out into the open sea, passing gigantic docks, huge cruise ships, the impressive coast guard base, the vast oil terminal and finally, the proud San Felippe del Morro Castle. Now nothing but the horizon separates us from our destination. A light breeze pushes us forward gently, riply wavelets are burbling along our bright orange hull, glittering in the Caribbean sun. Our destination is Marina Puerto Bahia on the Samana peninsula in the Dominican Republic. A short 200 nautical miles sail – just two days and two nights. As we leave the channel, we turn port to WNW on a beam reach course, heading straight for Samana. A perfect sailing day, relaxed and quiet.

It is so relaxed and quiet that Tom falls asleep on the foredeck, my boat dogs Cap'n Jack and Scout snooze in the cockpit, snuggled up tightly, and I am drifting away listening to my favorite audiobook. Only the auto-pilot is doing its work untiringly, keeping us on course as if we are gliding on magic rails.

Relaxed sailing: humans

Relaxed sailing: canines

When Tom wakes up later and I make some dinner, he is a little disappointed about the meager mileage covered and our current speed that barely exceeds three knots. But the sunset is beautiful and well rested as he is, he agrees to take the first night watch while I nestle down in my bunk without the slightest premonition of the price tag this negligence is going to have.

As usual, I fall asleep fast. We solo-sailors are able to sleep wherever and whenever we have the opportunity because they are rare. But as always a part of me stays awake, subconsciously listening to the sound of the wind and the waves and sensing the boat‘s movements. I feel a breeze on my face. I like it. It is hot in the cabin and the breeze feels good!

But a breeze? A *BREEZE*? Argh, this means I forgot to close the hatches! I must have forgotten to close them before we weighed anchor. Damnit! But I am way too lazy to get up, so I just enjoy the breeze and keep sleeping. I will close them when I get up for my watch.

"Five knots, five and a half!," Tom's excited voice breaks my sweet dreams.

We are heeling a little and the well audible whooshing confirms his announcements.

"Six, six and a half!"

For a moment I feel like I am on board the German WWII submarine *U96* in the movie "The Boat", when they keep falling after they got hit by a depth charge in the Straits of Gibraltar. Tom's speed reports sound just like the submarine's chief engineer's diving depth reports that end with "I report obediently: Boat is uncontrollable."

"*BOAT IS UNCONTROLLABLE!*," it echoes in my head, exactly in the moment when Tom cheers "Seven knots, yieeeha!"

7.5 knots is *Seefalke's* hull speed if I remember it correctly. She is not supposed to go faster than seven knots. She is not DESIGNED to go faster than seven knots through the water! The heeling has gotten to an unhealthy 30 degree tilt, maybe more. I have trouble jumping out of my bunk.

Through the unbearable noise of the howling wind I scream: "Tom, slack the sheets!"

When I finally stand on my feet with one on the wall and one on the bunk, tightly gripping the ceiling handrail while desperately trying to gain enough stability to move out of the cabin and into the cockpit, it knocks me over and off my feet completely. The wall becomes the floor, the aisle becomes the new wall as water is hitting me in the face, shooting through the open hatches so brutally and vehemently I have the feeling it pushes my eyes deep into my skull. I lose sight, the noise is deafening and I can hardly breathe. I get a little glimpse of how it must be to drown. Not peaceful at all!! I spit salty water. Somehow, and I do not remember how, I make it into the cockpit, desperately hoping Tom is still there.

And yes, he is, standing on the cockpit's sidewalls grasping to the steering wheel in despair. Finally, after what seems like an eternity but cannot have been more than a few seconds, I reach the cleats and tear loose the sheets, main first then genoa. Immediately the boat comes upright and the sound of the slapping sails becomes unbearable. I need to take the genoa down or it will tear like toilet paper. The boiling sea is black with green and red froth reflecting the spooky shine of the nav lights.

Nightfall

With nothing on but my underpants, no time to put on a life vest or a PLB (Personal Life Beacon), I carefully crawl forward on all fours to the foredeck, sliding wildly with *Seefalke* performing her worst rodeo. I hear myself talking to her to calm her down. Uncounted bangs and bruises later I make it to the halyard. It takes some effort and some risky maneuvering to tame and take down this large fabric, but eventually I get it done. But not before the large shackle at the sail tack lands a good swing on my face leaving me with a split lip, a tooth less and a mouthful of blood. It hurts badly but there is no time for pity right now. It could have been worse and hit me in the eye, for example. So I spit out the tooth and swallow the blood. Or was it the other way around? I don't know.

When I turn around to crawl back aft, I get hit by more spume smacking over the sea fence. Blood, sweat and tears are running down my face, and instinctively I think of Churchill and his historic speech. Still giggling of amusement and beginning madness, I slide back into the safe and dry cockpit and haul in the main sheet, finally regaining control over this vessel.

"Holy Moly," I think, "that was a close call!"

And I sit down and try to relax holding my swollen and bloody mouth. Cap'n Jack peers up to me as if he wanted to ask if it is safe now. So I nod down the companionway, his signal that it is ok to come up. But where is the other one? Where is Scout? I cannot see her in the main cabin where she was snuggled up to me under my blanket sleeping before the hell broke loose. I feel panic coming up. If she had gone overboard during the knockdown she is history. No way to find her pitch black body in the pitch black night in the pitch black water. No chance! Not the slightest. Anything else is sheer delusion. But hope dies last so I go down into the main cabin. I had not seen her coming up earlier, but really I do not know. Maybe she just hid somewhere, crawled deeper under the blanket or underneath the bunk or into the stern cabin. As I step down the rear companionway into the stern cabin I see the reflection of her eyes in the very stern, snuggled up to the spare sails and lines. Relief! As I come closer with my flashlight I see the cushion underneath her is wet. No blood, no sweat and also no tears, but it is ok. The accident is just fine! She is fine! Good girl! I take her in my arms and hold her tiny shivering body tight as we slowly move back into the cockpit where Cap'n Jack welcomes her back to life.

Logbook entry 2400hrs: "*Wind NE to ENE force 6 gusting 9, seas 7 ft increasing 10 ft, heavy rain, got knocked down in squall line, boat ok, crew ok, no visible damages, genoa reefed away, proceeding under mainsail only, HDG 295, COG 285, SOG 4.2 kts. Maik on watch.*"

When I make the midnight entry into the logbook I see Tom is still sitting there, motionless, pale, with empty eyes. I understand how he feels. He thinks it was his fault that I lost a tooth, I almost went overboard, we almost lost a dog and we almost capsized, because he hauled in the sheets rather than slack them during the fierce gusts. But it is not. Not at all. It was all my fault.

I hug him and I apologize. I apologize for not briefing him properly about the perniciousness of tropical squalls. I apologize for not reefing at sunset as I usually do. I apologize that I did not shut the hatches when we weighed the anchor. Three absolutely inexcusable mistakes that almost cost a ship, two human and two canine lives.

This is what I recall as I stand in the Apple service shop in Leipzig, Germany when the young computer specialist breaks the news to me that my MacBook Pro (newest generation) is a total write-off. In fact, it is beyond that. Neither him nor anyone else in the shop had ever seen anything like it. The laptop was in its case during the incident but a few drops of salt water made it inside. It still looks new from the outside but inside there is not a single component left that is not completely corroded or salt frozen. He says the repair would be 4,000 EUR but a new one would only be 2,000 EUR.

My crew for the passage from Puerto Rico to Dominican Republic

I think of the five lives that we didn't lose that night, and I think to myself, all in all, I got a good deal here. In fact, that $3,000 gust seems like quite a bargain...

So I take a photo of the wreck for my story and leave the store with a smile.

Squall Casualty

From Puerto Rico to the Dominican Republic

This was one of the most hurtful and most effective lessons in my entire sailing career. And the irony is, I did not learn anything new at all. It was all about things I already knew: Of course, you need to close the hatches, especially on an offshore passage at night. Of course, you need to reef for the night, especially in tropical waters and single-handing or - as in this case - with an inexperienced crew. And, of course, you need to brief that inexperienced crew of the specific features of the sea area you are navigating. All this is sailing 101.

But in reality there is distraction and self-confidence and one more ingredient that makes things dangerous: Exhaustion. Exhaustion makes you forget or at least suppress what you know. Exhaustion makes you underestimate risks. Exhaustion is the solo sailor's biggest enemy. Despite the relaxed start of the last passage, the remainder, after our night squall experience, was pretty challenging, too. The wind shifted from beam reach to almost head-on and the current was not in our favor either.

But finally we made it into the fancy marina of Puerto Bahia on the Samana Peninsula in the Dominican Republic. It is part of a guarded community that separates the rich from the less fortunate population.

I prefer the jungle over the zoo and so Tom and I and the two dogs ventured out to see places that the local dockmaster, visibly proud of his backyard, recommended to us. We took a taxi into town and frankly, we were quite shocked about the price. I assume when you are docked in rich white-man communities, you just need to pay rich white-man's rates. I swore to myself that this would have been the first and the last time.

You only Live Twice

"2,000 Pesos," the boy claims with great self-confidence.

He has a neon-yellow colored Iroquois hair style and his skin color is evidence of his creole heritage. He wears colorful shorts, flip-flops and a muscle shirt that dramatically reveals his tattoo, showing a – let's say – slightly underdressed girl with an impressive bust size. The detail that immediately catches my eyes, however, is that this girl similarly has a tattoo showing an Iroquois biker. Determined not to pay what I consider blunt robbery, I resolutely shake my head and make my counter offer, not less impertinent than his:

"500 Pesos, and not a single Centavo more!" He smiles the don't-bullshit-a-bullshitter smile. I respond with my sweetest don't-trick-your-brother smile.

My 17-year old son Tom taps me on my shoulder:

"Maybe we should try one more time to get a taxi? I mean the kind with four wheels."

Skeptically, he eyeballs the vintage and obviously brutally over-tuned motorcycle and its colorful rider. He is not worried about the price for the ride. He thinks what I think:

"How should the four of us plus him fit on his Suzuki moto-taxi and take a 10 mile ride through the mountains?" And Tom sure is not the kind of guy who gets worried too easily.

Exploring Samana Peninsula

The four of us are, besides my son and myself, my two boat dogs Cap'n Jack and Scout, two beagles that have traveled four continents on my sailboat. They have never ridden a motorcycle in their short lives, though. They still look happy because they simply do not have a clue of the matter of our negotiation. Sometimes not knowing is a blessing.

We have been roaming the province town Santa Barbara de Samana, or short just Samana, to find a taxi for more than an hour now without success. I have a phone number of the taxi service that brought us here from the marina but their prices were blunt robbery, and I would rather crawl on all fours through the jungle than to pay them another Centavo. Just the fact that our sailboat *Seefalke* is docked in the only marina in the area, inside a shotgun guarded, white-rich-man community, is reason enough to charge us ridiculous shot-gun guarded, white-rich-man rates.

The destination of my desire is Playa El Valle, one of the beaches that the harbormaster strongly recommended as one of the must-see-places in the area. He is a Samana Peninsula native and visibly proud of his backyard. He really got excited when he was talking about all the fun things to see around here. So, I am determined to go to Playa El Valle, and this Suzuki Iroquois seems to be my only way. I ask him again if he really is convinced we can all fit on his vehicle. His gestures speak more than a thousand words: He noisily revs the engine, shrugs innocently and smiles knowingly. Then he asks me if I think that four horses per passenger, the four-legged ones included, wouldn't be enough. I don't know why but this answer didn't take away my doubts completely. His bike looks like a Suzuki GN125 to me, mid 1980s made maybe. If I remember correctly they made the engine with ten horsepower. Doing the math he must have tuned it up times two. I am actually getting slightly more worried, much less considering the absence of helmets or other safety gear. So I make him an offer that I hope he will refuse:

"Brother, I'll pay you 1,000 Pesos but we need two bikes. I am ok with dying here and now but I have a responsibility for these three here, you understand?"

He nods compassionately. In his look I recognize pity for my burden of responsibility. Then his sharp whistle drowns out the traffic noise and another biker sets out toward us from the other side of the potholed three-and-a-half lane main street of Samana. We finally agree on 1,200 Pesos, 600 for each. Tom asks me with a smirk:

"Shouldn't it be us who get paid for this?" Oh, I am such a bad dad!

So, Tom gets the little one, Scout, and I take Cap'n Jack as we climb on the two motorcycles starting what we think will be our lives' last ride... the crossing of Styx, the journey to the Happy Hunting Ground. Now the dogs seem to understand the seriousness of the situation as they kick their legs like in a dog-karate contest. We grab the panicking canines tight like a screw clamp leaving us with limited ability to hold on to the two-wheeled kamikaze machines taking off like rockets.

I am just happy that neither Tom's mother nor my former first mate and owner of my two boat dogs are here to see this. In fact, if one of you two are reading this right now, I strongly recommend that you stop right here, as to continue may cause physical harm like a heart attack or nervous breakdown.

We soon begin weaving through the chaotic traffic of Samana... around pot-holes, wrecks and donkey carts, through narrow alleys, busy streets and dirt roads, past markets, lottery shops and unfinished and long forgotten buildings out of the city and up into the mountains. I learn why speed bumps are actually called "speed bumps": Well ahead of the bump you need to speed up and lift the front wheel to not bump into them, but hawk-like fly over them. The black tire stripes on the tarmac after each speed bump mark the current records of this informal long jump competition. With our overloaded vehicle we won't break any records, but surprisingly we *do* collect some flight time. The first speed bump catches me totally by surprise, though. I expect my driver to do what I would have done, which would be to slow down, carefully crawl over it and then accelerate again. But the opposite is the case. When he accelerates, the enormous g-forces brutally push me backward. Pressing Cap'n Jack on my chest with both hands, it's only my legs clamping us to the bike and keeping us from being catapulted underneath the vintage truck racing right behind us. I see the truck driver's excited grin, revealing his golden tooth twinkling in the sun, and I feel his hot breath in my sweat-soaked neck. Ehm, no, the hot air is actually coming from the overheated engine that is pushed beyond all reasonable limits. When the front wheel loses ground contact I feel my thighs merging with the seat, developing over-humanly strength, and when we finally go airborne I see Cap'n Jack rising higher and higher until, like in zero gravity, he is floating past my face right over my head. In slow motion I reach out to him, grab him in midair and pull him back on my chest right in time before the bike touches down with screeching tires, a good meter short of the black stripe marking the local record. I hear my Iroquois rider swear in disappointment. I get the feeling it is his own record that we just missed.

I don't have time to relax or even breathe deeply because the bike is swerving suddenly, right towards a girl walking on what is supposed to be the curb. From what I see from behind, it is one of those Caribbean goddesses: chocolate colored skin, long black hair, moving her voluptuous curves with naturally-born grace, effectively enhanced by hula-hoop size earrings and a super-tight super-short neon-pink stretch dress. I haven't seen her from the front yet but I know it would just perfect the picture. So does my driver. I think to myself:

"No, he is not going to do this! No, he cannot possibly want to do this!" And as we come as close as an arm's length to her well-proportioned body I clearly hear that kind of smack when a male hand spanks a female booty over the almost unbearable noise of the engine. He really did it!

"¡Cuando regrese, me voy a casar contigo!," (When I return I am going to marry you!) my intrepid friend proposes to her as we fly by.

When I turn around smiling my most apologetic smile I expect an angry woman, cursing us with all her power but she just smiles back, amused, obviously content with the effect her body has on passing bikers. As I am still wondering if I just witnessed a Dominican blitz engagement and by default turned into my driver's best man, I hear my son's voice:

"Hey papa! Are you having fun yet?" as they are taking advantage of our slight detour to one of the Seven Wonders of the World and pass us with death-defying speed.

Oh, shit, the race is on now. Everything till now was just a warm-up.

We accelerate as well, and reach the first mountaintop almost at the same time. The view over the jungle is breathtaking.

"At least I'll die seeing something beautiful," I think to myself, but I am not scared anymore.

For now, I just want to win this race. Our lives are just a fair price to pay for it.

At least I die seeing something beautiful

On the way downhill our drivers turn off the engine. It turns quiet for a while. Just the wind is howling in my ears as we get faster and faster rolling down the winding road in heart-stopping free-fall. We all cuddle up and duck down to be as aerodynamic as possible. Only Cap'n Jack's head is sticking out like a brake flap, creating unnecessary air friction, the literal dog in the manger. I take a peek at the speedometer and it shows zero, obviously not quite correct, but I am kind of happy about it. I don't really want to know. I think I see it before my driver does: On the valley bottom there is something shimmering, silvery. Is this water? Or just tarmac reflecting the sun?

"Holy Moly, it is water," I think.

As we come closer I can confirm it is a huge puddle. It had rained the past few days, it makes sense. I can only speculate how deep it is. But I am positive we will find out in a few moments, one way or the other. There is no way around it and we passed the safe braking distance light years ago. My friend is trying to crank the engine just as we are about to test our amphibious abilities. I can only hope he knows what he is doing. The motor starts a millisecond before we hit that road pond in a ginormous splash. Surprisingly we get less wet than I expected, but we do get wet. Cap'n Jack is not happy and it takes all my strength to keep him from abandoning the sinking ship. I turn around and see Tom and his bike. They were less lucky as they were fully hit by our wake. I see his driver grimly looking at us, thirst for revenge sparkling in his eyes, water dripping from his angry face. My pilot and I high-five as we are ascending the next mountain.

Playa El Valla - worth the ride

As we descend the next steep road down into another valley there is a sudden, deafening bang that shakes our bike badly. It only takes a split second for my creole Iroquois to regain control and we stop at the side of the road. The chain snapped. Obviously not his first time. Cesar, that is actually the name of our driver, gets it fixed in a few minutes and off we go again.

A few minutes later and against all odds we make it to the beach. All six of us. Alive. It better be worth it. When I get off the bike, I kiss the dogs, I hug Tom and I shake Cesar's hand, thanking him for the extremely fast and extraordinarily safe ride, and for taking such good care of us on land, on water and in the air. Who wants to live forever anyway?

When he asks if they should wait for us to take us back to town, I see Tom's eyes, silently begging me to turn down this honestly well-meant offer. Tom might be right. You only live twice.

So, as a gentleman I selflessly release Cesar of his obligations:

"You better get back to your fiancé, bro, and close the deal!"

From the Dominican Republic to the Bahamas

I know that this story features attitudes and behaviors that are uncommon for most of us. It even got rejected by some travel magazines for being not "politically correct". Especially the intrepid encounter with the Caribbean goddess appeared to be the stumbling block. But this is not fiction. I tell the stories as they were. Here and there I am using means of literature to emphasize a certain scene but the main plot, the core of the story, is always true. The whole reason I travel is to see and experience things that are different from home, that are different from what I already know. To accept and take the unknown with humor always seemed to be the best approach. So, to make it clear, I do not endorse sexist behavior, I simply accept that things are different in different parts of the world and I do not see it as my mission to evangelize the world with our western view.

However, Tom and I had a great time in the Dominican Republic and he was not too keen to return to his second home Alabama. Before I set sail to Great Inagua, the southernmost of the Bahamian islands, I got permission by the Dominican navy to visit Los Haitises National Park which was absolutely amazing. Mountains, covered with tropical rainforest, reaching into the sea, dolphins playing, parrots flying, and I had all that completely for myself. But at one point it was time for me to go to sea again and leave this little paradise in my wake.

Seefalke in Haitises National Park

The most exciting experience while sailing the seven seas are the encounters with people from other worlds. From worlds so far from ours they might as well have just landed from Mars. Sometimes their stories are sad, sometimes they are funny, but they are almost always inspiring. Some of the most memorable encounters I had in Great Inagua, Bahamas during my visit in December 2019. The first time I ever heard about an island called Great Inagua was, when I charted my route from Samana, Dominican Republic to Florida. It was right on the way and seemed to be a perfect stop. However, my up-to-date Navionics and C-Map charts said the small harbor of Matthew Town was under construction and not accessible. I finally decided to go there anyway, first, there was a user comment somewhere saying the construction is complete and second, in case it was not, I would just drop my anchor outside. I planned for a short stop to clear in and continue my voyage to Florida. But things should turn out very differently.

Great Inagua, the southernmost and maybe least typical Bahamian island, is not blessed with white beaches or tourist attractions. In fact, the landscape is rough and reminds me of my home in the Baltic Sea. Most of the island (300,000 acres) is used by Morton Salt for the second largest saline operation in North America, producing 1,000,000 pounds of salt per year. Then there are wild donkeys and flamingos and a beautiful light house and – there are the approximately 1,000 Inaguans, the friendliest people in the Caribbean.

There is harbormaster George, the most helpful person you can imagine. With his limited resources on this remote island he will try to make your stay as comfortable and enjoyable as possible. Any wish that is fulfillable, you can be sure that he knows someone that can help you, and he will be on the phone before you even finish your sentence. Once I ask him if there was a bike rental on the island. He says:

"Unfortunately not, once there was one, but he moved away."

His disappointment visibly is even worse than mine when I turn around and return to my boat. Two days later, it is past 0100hrs, I wake up from the loud and vehement barks of my boat dogs Cap'n Jack and Scout. So I finally get up and check out the cause of this infernal noise. There is this guy on the dock, and he says:

"I brought you a bike."

My brains do not function quite yet and obviously it shows. He says again:

"I brought you a bike. My brother in law said you needed a bike."

And it is true, he has a bike with him that he puts right next to *Seefalke*. Now fully awake we have a little post-midnight chat on the dock. He is George's brother in law and lobster fisher. He is waiting for his partner and they intend to go out to the offshore sand banks and hunt some lobster, he will be gone for three days, and while he is gone I can use his bike. I am confused and overwhelmed by this kindness and generosity but eventually he convinces me that this is just what they do here on the island. And he tells me more about his lobster hunting tours, too.

So they go out to the offshore sandbanks in a tiny open boat. This is where the lobsters are, the big ones. They anchor their boat, go in the water and catch them with slings. In the night they put up their tent either on the beach or on a sandbank, depending on where they are. Then they have some lobster barbecue on an open fire and continue the next day until the three giant cool boxes are full. Two with lobsters, one with a conch. He says they can sell it for 15 USD a pound in Great Inagua or 20 USD in Nassau, so this is what they prefer. He expects a catch of 300-400 pounds. And it is true, when he comes back a few days later, their cool boxes are stuffed to the rim with lobster tails. And they have sold half of them before they even finished tying up the boat.

And then there is Tara, a school teacher in the local high school who also offers tours through the island and the national park. One day I get a text message from Tara asking if I would be available this afternoon at 1630hrs to be taken through town. I do not have much better to do, reply "Yes, wonderful!" and on time at 16:30hrs a Jeep is pulling up to the dock and Tara gets out. She welcomes me as if we have been friends forever, in fact we see each other for the first time. Then she takes us (Jo joined us, a solo sailor who arrived a few days past me) through the streets of Matthew Town. She is a Great Inaguan native, born and raised here and never really left. She knows everybody and everybody knows her. She shows us all the restaurants that mainly consist of an additional table in some people's living rooms and would have been difficult to find without her help, and where and when the local parties will be. She tells us the story about the first Bahamian prison that not too long ago was burnt down in a riot. She tells us about the primary and high schools that for their 1,000 population have 150 students. I am quite impressed, but I understand...

She tells us how almost everything here is owned by Morton Salt and how they wished to have more tourists. We drive out to the ponds to see the flamingos and to the beautiful lighthouse. We have a drink at her friend's house before we get back to the dock when it is already dark. When I ask her how much we owe her for this excursion she just shakes her head.

"Just tell people about us," she says.

This is just for you to understand what kind of place Great Inagua is.

I first thought it was a joke when the next morning after my arrival I asked George where immigration would be. He replies:

"It is a ten minute walk up that road but I am sure they won't let you walk."

So I get my documents and head off to the immigration building. And like George said, I have not gone 200 yards when a white Jeep is pulling up next to me. A man in khaki uniform says:

"I guess you want to see me. Get in!"

It turns out it is Pratt, the immigration director. He takes me to the customs office and tells me to come to see him after I am finished with them. So I fill in all the paperwork to get my permit and walk next door to immigration. After the formalities are done we talk a lot. About Germany and how much he wants to travel to Europe but is afraid of racism. I never was aware that Europe had such a bad reputation. And we talk about Haitian refugees, and how this is his biggest headache at the moment. The Bahamian authorities patrol the waters together with the US Coast Guard and almost every week they bring Haitian refugees to Great Inagua. They first register and finger print them and keep them in the police station's garage until they bring them back. He tells me if they come again, then they are being brought to Nassau and charged with illegal border crossing. He says the saddest part is that they consider the four weeks in Nassau prison a step up from where they are coming from. Having a shelter and food three times a day is more than they have back in Haiti. This short and friendly officer with his huge Colt visibly struggles with his official task on the one side and his compassion with those poor guys simply seeking a better life on the other, which is what the next story is about.

The Brave Men of *La Patience*

When I landed in Matthew Town, Bahamas I pulled up to the loading dock but the next day I had to move to one of the wooden small craft docks because the "cargo ship" was expected and supposed to take my spot. As I am busy moving my boat to the assigned spot in the gusting winds all by myself, I see a sailboat anchored a few cables away from the harbor entry. I think:

"Oh, other sailors, cool!"

They probably arrived at night and waited for sunlight to pull in. Then I see them hoist their sails and head for the harbor entry. Next thought, those must be real sailors, or their engine is just broken. They put out their oars and row this heavy wooden boat into the harbor to the loading dock where they finally tied her up. I do what we do in the cruising world and walk over there to say hello. As I come closer I see the poor condition this boat is in. It is a wooden sailboat that looks as though it was recently recovered from wreckage. The mast is a cricket tree, with just the branches being cut off and so is the boom. The galley is an open fire pit on the deck, the water tank a blue open barrel and the only navigational equipment a bare compass. No engine, no life-vests, no gps... The crew of five look exhausted but also relieved and happy. Communication is difficult, but soon I find out they are trade sailors from Haiti. So I decide to talk to the captain and invite them for a barbecue this evening.

The "galley" of La Patience

I buy wagon loads of buns and patties and cheese and other burger supplies and in the evening I carry my grill over and we have a decent barbecue right on the loading dock. Communication is still difficult. Their English is poor, their French full of Creole which doesn't make it easier. However we have so much fun, we share our burgers with Cap'n Jack and Scout and I learn a lot about their homes and lives.

La Patience under sail

Their home is the Pirate Haven Tortuga, which today is part of Haiti. Haiti, the poorest of the Caribbean countries was knocked out by the earthquake and almost annihilated by the following hurricanes. The coast guards of the surrounding countries are constantly busy fishing Haitian refugees out of the sea. Yet not my friends! They recovered a wreck and made it float. They buy agricultural produce in Haiti and sail it to Great Inagua in the Bahamas to sell it which is a 1-2 days voyage. Then they wait for the mail ship to send money to their families in Nassau. They take orders from the locals for the new run and then they set sail again. They sleep on a big mattress on the deck. They cook on an open fire pit. They have no shelter from the weather because all the room down below is needed for cargo.

But they are happy because they make a living. They can support their families and do not need to run away, embarrassed, to be disgracefully picked up by the coast guard and put into camps. Never in my life have I seen people so poor so motivated and enthusiastic about pulling themselves out of poverty into a better life.

The mast is a cricket tree

During the few days they were here we talked a lot and when they left this morning, my phone number was written in bright red letters on their mattress. If they call me, I will visit them in Tortuga, Haiti on my way south.

These are my heroes. They are the hope of Haiti. And when life punches me in the face next time, I will remember the brave men of *La Patience.*

La Patience in Matthew Town

Mattress on deck

From the Bahamas to Cuba

We left Great Inagua, Bahamas on December 28th, 2019 around 1300hrs with some delay because I needed to climb the mast to cut the tangled Christmas lights off the rigging. However we set sail and the forecasted force five quickly turned into a force six to seven (near gale force) and the 10 ft waves of the forecast rather looked (and felt) like 16 ft to me.

Anyway, I met my friend Jo on *Cool Breeze* who left Great Inagua three hours ahead of us and very soon I lost sight of her. She was bound for Florida, too, to the Gulf side, though. So we had charted the same general course. *Seefalke* and I were flying northwest, got a bad beating but made good time. Before VHF communication with *Cool Breeze* was lost, the last transmission indicated there was a problem on *Cool Breeze*, however not serious enough that it required immediate assistance. So we agreed that we would wait for them on the other side of the front in the forecast calm.

After two days, finally, we had passed the weather and as if someone pushed a button, the furious Atlantic turned into a peaceful, innocent pond. It reminded me a little of one of Cap'n Jack, when he put on his most innocent dog-look saying "No, it wasn't me! Can these eyes lie?"

So I hove-to in order to keep my waiting position and enjoyed the calm after the storm. This gave me the opportunity to clear the mess in the cabin that was caused by my temporarily installed refrigerator being catapulted through the boat, uncontrollably unloading its entire content on the cabin floor. Pie was dripping from the head door, a melange of eggs, ketchup and milk turned the floor into slimy, slippery grounds -it was a dogs' paradise and skipper's hell. I must admit they did a great job cleaning the mess, though!

Atlantic disguised as innocent pond

Running low on propane I could even make lunch in our solar oven and enjoy the first hot meal in days. New Year's Eve went past and the New Year started with a clear horizon. No sail, no sign of *Cool Breeze*, though. Finally I received an eight digit call-back number on my satellite phone, which made no sense. But after I translated this assumed call-back number into a geographical position it could well be that *Cool Breeze* was still around 60 nautical miles behind. Later it turned out Jo could not send satellite text message so she used this trick to submit her position. So finally, on the evening of January 1st, SAILS ON THE HORIZON!

We established a line connection, I swam over and we had dinner together after which I returned to *Seefalke* and we cut the line connection. The rest of the night we would just drift and get some well needed sleep.

It turned out in the bad weather a huge breaking sea slammed into *Cool Breeze's* cockpit and flooded the electrical installation below. Two batteries had to be cut off and the remainder of power was not enough to run the auto-pilot, so Jo was manually steering for almost four days! We agreed we would proceed the next morning and try to stay within VHF range. Needless to say that *Cool Breeze's* VHF antenna was blown off and "VHF range" now meant "handheld VHF range" which is not more than three nautical miles.

Still headed for Florida the next day I received a gale warning for the Strait of Florida with gale force northerly winds. So we decided to sail northwest instead and call in Varadero, Cuba and wait for better weather there. From here it is just 80 nautical miles to Key West, Florida.

We finally arrived in Varadero on January 4th around noon, so exactly 7 days after our departure. The reception was most friendly and the clearance procedure time-consuming but pleasant. Customs, immigration, coastguard, customs veterinarian and pet veterinarian one after another boarded *Seefalke* and checked every compartment and locker. GPS devices, satellite phones, emergency flares and rockets were sealed but finally the boat, the dogs and me were cleared to enter Gaviota Marina, with 1,350 slips the largest marina of the northern Caribbean, however apart from some local boats we were just the third visitor of this season. Due to the unfortunate bilateral political tensions the marina is lacking their target clients: US sailors.

So, welcome to the Ghost Marina!

Ghost Marina

Most sailors dream of sailing the Caribbean at least once in their lives. They dream of warm weather, clear water, secluded anchorages, and endless beaches... The reality hits them with unaffordable marinas, crowded anchorages and crazy labor rates. I am not saying there are no hidden gems left off the beaten path anymore but the beaten path has become a beaten autobahn in recent decades, an industry aggressively aiming at the cruisers' pockets.

So wouldn't it be just great if there was an affordable marina with all possible amenities, spacious and safe, in the center of popular cruising grounds? At mooring fees less than 50 cents per foot per day? With free 110V/220V shore power for each slip, free water, wifi, plenty of showers and bathrooms, swimming pool, laundry, cafes and restaurants and even a shuttle bus to the next city? With a competent boat yard, 100 ton-travel lift, huge and hurricane safe hard storage, sailmaker, specialized welding and motor workshops that offer their competent services for less than 20 USD per hour? With a dedicated customs pier and crew, a marina traffic control tower, towing service and security guards? And the wonderful beach just a few minutes walk away?

And here I am, walking through a deserted, fairly new, 5-star marina. Yet, I am walking past empty slips and lonely mooring balls. Usually the boats are supposed to med-moor stern in but the few visitors have all gone alongside the endless finger piers. Five years ago the marina was extended to its current size of an unbelievable 1350 transient slips and an additional 100 slips for local (mostly charter) boats, making it one of the largest marinas in the Caribbean. Yet, today, as I keep walking through the perfectly landscaped premises, I count five visiting boats: four compatriots from Germany and one Columbian boat that only came in for a mechanical.

Ghost marina Gaviota

When I arrived, the dockmaster and the entire immigration, customs and veterinarian crew would already be waiting for me at the conveniently laid-out customs pier. The customs building, exclusively built for international marina visitors can easily compete with that of many international airports and is designed to process 100 arrivals per day.

On the wild and rough passage Seefalke's boom-mast connection finally sheered off. It needs to be welded urgently. When I bring my boom to the boatyard's workshop they immediately start working. Two mechanics are taking loving care of my boom, and two hours later it is – no kidding – better than new! When I get the bill a few days later, they charge me the equivalent of 18 USD.

There is no need to show the little card they gave me when I pass the security checkpoints on my way past the main plaza to the main gate. They know me. 15 minutes later I am at a stunning beach. Very touristy, but also plenty of activities: windsurfing, sea kayaking, kite surfing, cat sailing, snorkelling,... you name it! Tourists are plenty, but where are all the sailors?

When I walk back to the marina, I am humming

"Where have all the sailors gone?" to the tunes of that old Woodstock song.

Where have all the sailors gone?

And I really do not understand. A few miles north it is hard to get a spot in a marina even though the fees are ten times higher. And a few miles east sailors easily pay 300 USD for just a cruising permit.

Customs pier in Varadero

In the evening the wind is picking up to near gale force. When I am on the pier making sure my lines and my fenders are ok, I hear dockmaster Francisco's friendly, cigar blurred voice

"¡Hola, amigo!"in the dark.

As we chat a few minutes while we have coffee I learn that the marina management has ordered special night shifts for the dockmasters due to the weather. They are supposed to do hourly rounds to check on everyone's lines and fenders. I am still flabbergasted about their customer friendly attitude when he has left.

Back on my boat my thoughts take wing and fly: With a little bit of marketing and word of mouth this place would flourish! I know sailors from all over the world would love this place! But then my thoughts turn bitter, as always when sailing meets politics: Imagine, this place was not blacklisted by the US Treasury Department. Imagine, US sailors would not be deprived of their freedom to travel here. This place would be a place full of life! A place where sailors from all over the world meet and exchange stories and make new friends and can rest.

Welcome to Marina Gaviota, Varadero, Cuba!

From Cuba to the USA

While we enjoyed Cuba I almost forgot that I was on a mission. I promised to deliver the dogs from Suriname to my first landfall in the United States mainland, and the United States mainland was now just 90 nautical miles away. So it became time to prepare the boat for this passage. Just 90 miles but the emotionally toughest 90 miles of the entire voyage. While I was waiting for a good weather window the girls from customs were working on their wish list.

I think I did not tell you that when I arrived I docked at the customs pier as I was supposed to. The very friendly Port Captain welcomed me to Cuba and two sweet angels in their sexy Cuban uniforms boarded my boat. One was immigration and one customs. Let me be honest, I did not complain that it took so long. But in a moment of distraction I dropped my pen that I used to fill in the gazillion forms. This is when the fatal calamities took their course. Naturally, I dove to the floor to pick up my lost treasure coming dangerously close to those endless legs in that filigrane black lace pantyhose. As a gentleman, of course, I tried not to take advantage of this unfortunate situation and looked the other way. A fatal mistake! Not only because I deprived myself of this visual delicacy but even more so because I was not able to fully control the route my pen would take on the way up to surface. And there the disaster happened: first a ripping whoosh, then a bloodcurdling scream and I saw the run, longer than most people's legs. Despite my sunburnt complexion I blushed like a school boy and gibbered some muttered apologies. The girl took off her stockings right there, only with utmost difficulty holding back her tears. Eventually I could calm her down mentioning that I will travel to Florida in a week and that I would come back and bring her all the stockings she could dream of.

And while I waited for a good weather window, my young, long-legged friends from immigration and customs and the anti-drug department and the veterinarian and the dock master's daughter and the Port Captain's wife were working on their wish-list. Finally, when the weather cleared, I set out to sea with my two dogs and a shopping list that could easily span the Straits of Florida, the entire customs crew waving me goodbye.

As nice as my departure was from Cuba, my arrival on the other side turned out to be terrible.

Not my Day

There are days in life when you are doomed to lose, when the shit just will not drop off your foot, and if you keep shaking it, it eventually lands on your face making a bad day even worse.

This is one of those days. The first half of the day was great. The passage from Cuba to Florida was bumpy but fast. I arrived around noon, found a vacant mooring ball of the City Marina's mooring field but from this moment events took a downward turn.

I get my dinghy ready to find the dinghy dock and check in with the dockmaster. But the outboard would not crank. I do what good mechanics do, give it a critical look including the use of loud and inadequate language which makes me seem even more professional. However, the outboard is little impressed so I punish it with negligence and replace it with my electrical baby, even though I suspect the ride a bit long for the battery. But the choice is limited and so off we go. (Did I mention I dropped my good knife into the water?)

The good news of the day is that: Eventually I find the dinghy dock and the dockmaster's office, just two nautical miles from the mooring buoy. Yet the next problem occurs when I want to pay for it. It turns out I lost my one and only working credit card, either I left it in the ATM in Cuba or in the middle of the Straits of Florida, both possibilities make it equally inaccessible. The other cards don't work because the banks had identified my excessive traveling pattern as fraud and keep sending new cards to my home address... which was where exactly?? So the only chance is to get cash from an ATM using my European EC-cards. Finally, after at least a marathon distance of walking I find an ATM that at least gives me 200 USD (daily limit?) out of one card.

Feeling like a king I return to the dockmaster to pay my due. Then I make the fatal mistake and check my emails. The most recent is a friendly note from the US Customs and Border Protection Agency (CBP) that "unfortunately my clearance has not been approved and I may not enter the US at this time". What the heck?? It may be useful to know that non-US sailors have to report each arrival to the US using the dedicated app provided by the US CBP, only the first time you have to see the authorities at a port of entry to have your visa and boat documents checked and obtain a cruising permit that is valid for a year. I did all that in Puerto Rico. The above email is the reply to me reporting my arrival in Key West. Theoretically, I wouldn't even be allowed to leave the boat. Too late for that anyway, I think and use the last bit of my shoes' soles to hike to the local CBP office.

Now here comes the funny part: some governmental buildings in the US do not permit cell phones to be brought in. So they ask me to hide it in the bushes in the front yard, mentioning the two black limousines on the curb, adding that I didn't need to hide it too well, as long as those limousines were there, nobody would go looking for it anyway. I do as I was told and "hide" my phone on the lawn in the front yard. Then I have a nice chat with the guys from CBP during which we all agree that my threat to the safety of their country is minimal, especially since I can't even rent a car without a credit card to show off my German autobahn driving skills. And so it is that my short time as an illegal immigrant is already history. With a stamp in my passport and the second smile on my face that day I leave the building, pick my phone like a flower and start my second marathon back to the dinghy dock.

And so the lonesome cowboy of the seas rides on his dinghy into the sunset. But only about 2-3 cables. The sunset comes faster than the dinghy wants to ride – battery dead. So I pick up my emergency paddle saving 6 months worth of gym money, paddle the dinghy back to the mothership, which was parked where exactly? Have you ever forgotten where you left your car in a dark parking lot? Welcome to my world!

I hope I wouldn't burn my hand when I'd sit down in the cockpit with a genuine Cuban cigar and celebrate the best part of this eventful day – its end.

Part Two:

Culture Clash

Home Leave

As you already know it was my current mission to bring the dogs back to the continental USA after my first mate signed off *Seefalke's* crew in Suriname. It is my pleasure to report that this emotionally and nautically challenging mission is now accomplished.

This crew change is the most difficult I ever had. The dogs have been on board from day one of this epic voyage and have an unbelievable record of 9,443 nautical miles and 251 days at sea. Few human sailors can compete with this record. They protected *Seefalke* north and south of the equator and east and west of the Atlantic. They sailed through furious storms and tenacious calms, through bitter cold and brutal heat. They never complained, however harsh the conditions might have been.

The best crew I ever had

The recent five months brought us even closer together as it was just the three of us. And when we finally set sail from Suriname beginning of November, for the last 2,270 nautical miles across the Caribbean Sea, we shared our food (most places we stopped do not sell dog food), our bowls (saved water), our beds, our ticks, the ups and lows, our fears and our pleasures.

Exploring the rainforest

Together we even survived a bad knock-down in an ugly thunderstorm. We explored beaches and waterfalls, hiked through jungles and prairies and made human and canine friends from all over the world. They fell overboard, were rescued, once stole all my cereals, helped themselves to the milk powder, and punished me by taking the trash apart when I was gone for too long as they thought.

Long story short, they were a fine crew, the best I ever had. Some may say the dogs are finally home, I say they just left it. Sailing is full of farewells. This is a hard one. As sad as I was to lose my canine companions, I finally felt free at last. No crew that I was responsible for, no dogs that I needed to take care of. I could go now wherever I wanted whenever I wanted and for how long I wanted.

And as of right now, I wanted to leave this place. Key West had bad energy for me. So, after the dog transfer was complete I took care of the Cuban shopping list as fast as I could and set sail again, back to Cuba. The weather was not favorable and I hadn't seen anything of the southernmost point of the United States but I rushed to leave this place. It felt good to see Florida fade behind the horizon.

And the next day, when I pulled up to the customs pier in Varadero, I felt like Santa Claus. The customs girls were already waiting for me, the boarding procedure went without incidents this time. They just found a lot of undeclared merchandise that I willingly allowed them to confiscate. Coincidentally the confiscated goods matched exactly the items on the wish list: stockings, razor blades, tooth brushes, tooth paste, lighters, apples, some steaks,... This place was so much more welcoming than Key West!

With the new freedom I could finally fly to Germany to catch up with some work and see friends and family, for the first time in more than six months. As wonderful as it was to be home as much I suffered from this blatant culture shock. It took me some time to get used to this pace, the efficiency and this rules abiding society. A different world entirely! And as much as I loved seeing my friends and my family and as much as I enjoyed the amenities of civilization I missed my boat even more.

A Legal Alien

"Uh oh, I'm an alien, I'm a legal alien....", Sting has been following me today from the moment I got out of the plane in Düsseldorf, Germany.

I just arrived from Cuba, where I left my boat and home *Seefalke* for two weeks to take care of some urgent business and admin in the fatherland.

Herds of grey suits form a faceless mass flowing down the endless aisles and hallways of this busy airport. Smartphones are flying by at head level, leaving a trace of mumble about deals and appointments and deadlines. Elevators and escalators continuously pump ties and skirts to the next level where they are efficiently scanned, sorted and processed to their final destination.

From the jungle...

... to civilization

I am just standing there a little lost in my ragged jeans, my worn-out, salty leather jacket and my sunburnt face. A small army backpack is my only luggage. For how long I don't know. It is probably a hundred deals and a thousand deadlines later when I finally start trudging to my gate. The waiting area is full of laptops and tablets and phones working towards a new GDP record. While I have my coffee I keep wondering: Where have all the people gone?

When I was last in Germany, it was at the height of summer, and the blistering sun made that part of the transition easy for me, having arrived from the brutal heat of Suriname's jungle. Now it is cold. Maybe not as cold as it could be at the end of January, but the temperatures leave little doubt it is winter. While I am waiting on the flight that should take me to Berlin, I remember that, back then, I had the same feeling of being a stranger in my own home country. I remember how I was walking through the streets of Frankfurt: How amazed I was that everything was available in decadent abundance. As I stand in front of a phone shop, I remember how I needed a case for my new iPhone XS while I was in Paramaribo, Suriname's lively capital, and how it took me two entire days to finally find a store that had one. Not a choice, just and only exactly one. How I almost kissed the saleslady and happily counted the bills on the counter and felt like a hero who successfully killed the dragon and can finally marry the princess. Mission accomplished. This little phone shop here in Frankfurt has more choices than there are in all Suriname! And a few doors down the street there is another one and another one...

I try to imagine how someone would feel coming here for the first time. Like Ithiel, a teenage boy who loved to hang out with me in Domburg. Domburg is a small town on the outskirts of Paramaribo. He was born and raised in a small remote Creole settlement in the center of Suriname. Neither roads nor airfields connect this village to 'civilization'. From there it takes an entire day and experienced canoe driving daredevils to overcome the malicious races to only make it to a place with a road connection. Back in the day it was this remoteness that saved the runaway slaves' lives. But today the jungle kids have smartphones, too and want to see the world. Now this kid, who dropped out of school and left the jungle village to make money to become a pilot, loved to ask me about the world. If people would go out if it was cold? And if the rain was cold, too? And he genuinely was impressed that there was compulsory schooling. (In Suriname most girls go to school only as long as they can avoid getting pregnant.)

I try to imagine Ithiel here in Frankfurt or Berlin or London or Chicago. I fail. Even though I have been away from the modern western world for quite some time now, living on my boat in mostly remote underdeveloped places, I still cannot deny my origin. My senses are still dull enough to survive this omnipresent stimulus overkill. But how would it affect the sensitive feelers of my Suriname jungle friend?

On my sailboat I have crossed oceans, fought furious storms, endured endless calms, and have ventured into uncharted waters and unknown lands. And mostly I did this solo... on my own. I take a lot of strength from this, and coolness. It lets peer pressure drop off me like spray from my dodger. But also it sometimes makes it difficult to fit back into society, even temporarily.

Not too long ago I met this solo sailing girl in the Bahamas, and one evening I decided to be a gentleman and take her out to dinner. The restaurant was a decent place and when we arrived there, I realized I wasn't wearing shoes. So I ran back to the boat to get my shoes. I forget to hold the door for the lady and fall on my chair before she even has reached hers. I'll spare the details of my non-existent table manners, shaped from countless meals at sea shared only with my seadogs. So, on the way home to the boat I promise myself I will always pretend to have company when I have meals on solo passages in the future. At least I want to make an effort.

My thoughts are interrupted suddenly by an angry voice calling my name. I look up and I see that all the suits and ties and phones and laptops are gone and it's only me left in the waiting area of the gate. I shoulder my backpack, and as I filter in through the narrow aisle to take my seat in the very back of the plane I hear the accusing chorus of the faceless mass. I finally wedge into my seat and cannot help smiling when I remember that in my previous life, I was one of them: a rat racing for its life. So being an alien is not so bad after all.

And as the plane takes off, I close my eyes and listen to Sting: "Uh oh I'm an alien, I'm a legal alien..."

I Am not a Sissy

It is winter. I am still in Germany. I have been here for almost two weeks and in less than two days I am going to fly back home to my boat *Seefalke*. She is in tropical Cuba now, waiting for me.

It is cold. Sabine just passed, a furious winter storm, but luckily it brought less damage than expected. I am waiting in line out on the apron of Frankfurt International Airport to board my flight to Prague to continue my speed dating run in the Czech Republic. The wind bites me in the face, I am shivering.

When the pilot makes his announcement I learn that the outside temperature is 4°C. 4°C, that is almost 40°F, I do the math in my head. That is not cold, really. At least not for mid February in Germany. Not for a latitude of 50° N that, on the American side, approximately corresponds to the one of Vancouver. Would the Canadians in British Columbia consider 40°F cold? I doubt it.

Then I remember times when I would not consider 40°F cold, either. I remember winter 2005/2006. I was on my way driving from Dresden, Germany to Krasnoe, a tiny village in Tver Region in Northwest Russia, visiting my sister-in-law together with my son Tom. I remember how it was cold already when I left Germany, below freezing. I took the ferry across the Baltic Sea from Rostock to Hanko in Finland, a twenty hour passage. I remember how we got stuck in ice on the approach to Hanko, an icebreaker had to clear the way to the harbor. I remember how I thought I freeze to death when I stood in line on the Finnish-Russian border. (You have to get out of the car and visit several kiosks to complete the extensive immigration formalities.) I remember it was -8°F (-22°C) when I finally got back in the car, cleared to enter the world's biggest country, not quite known for its welcoming climate. At 61°N it was the time of the arctic dusk. Or dawn, if you prefer to consider the glass half-full. When I passed the very familiar Saint Petersburg, the northernmost +1,000,000 city of the world, where once upon a time I was a student of the Technical University, the thermometer of the car outside showed -20°F (-29°C). And as we headed deeper into the white endlessness it dropped with every mile. It finally hit bottom when we crossed the state line from Pskov Region to Tver Region at -45°F (-43°C). -45°F! My personal cold record!!

Country road in Tver Region, Russia

Then I remember how all of a sudden I realized I hadn't seen a car in hours. No cell signal, either. What if the car broke down? What if the motor died? Not too unlikely thinking about my aged Ford Focus and the poor state of Russian country roads. It would mean the end. As simple as that. The only good news would be, it would go fast.

I got an idea of how fast exactly when my son Tom, three years old at the time, had to pee. So I formed a careful plan of this operation, had everything ready to reduce the time out in this hostile environment to an absolute minimum. Eventually I stopped the car with the motor running of course, opened the driver's door, ran around the trunk and pulled Tom's door open, grabbed him quickly and put him on the ground beneath the car and quickly opened his skiing-overall. He did what he had to do, but a few drops made it on his pants. I returned to the car, grabbed some tissues to fix it but at the time, it couldn't have been more than a few seconds, it was frozen to his pants. I could simply flick it off with my finger. This is how cold -45°F is..

After three days of travel we spent two weeks in my sister-in-law's old wooden Russian farm house with outside toilets, sleeping on mattresses on top of the fireplace, crushing the ice in the bucket in the kitchen to make tea in the mornings. In these two weeks it never got warmer than -18°F (-28°C), and that only in the roasting afternoon sun. We spent a big share of the time outside playing in the snow or ice skating on the nearby river.

And now I am complaining (to myself only of course) about a ridiculous 40°F? How soft did I get? I am shivering with embarrassment, I guess, it could be the cold that makes me shiver, though. I am not quite sure. Ok, I know all this stuff about chill factor and the impact of humidity. But still...

Our beautiful planet, despite being the only one in quite some astronomical distance to provide life-friendly conditions, is still a pretty hostile place. In fact there is only a very narrow belt in the tropics that allows human life without technical assistance. The rest is either too cold or too hot.

Cold

Talking about too hot... A few months ago, when I sailed the equatorial waters of Brazil, French Guiana and Suriname, there was a time I had forgotten what exactly "cold" was. And how "freezing" felt.

I remember one evening in Domburg, Suriname when I discussed with my good friends Steffi and Rolf, a German sailing couple whom I first met in French Guiana, about the permanent heat and the effects it had on our lives. The afternoons were the most brutal time of the day. Broiling in your own body juices it was almost impossible to do boat work or focus on anything. But it was too hot to sleep, too. Skin funguses and mosquitoes were the only living organisms flourishing in this climate, it seemed.

Hot and humid

My young friend Ithiel from a Creole jungle village, who had never left Suriname and dreamt of traveling the world, was only afraid of two things: racism and cold. He kept asking me how we could live with four different seasons, how we would know how to dress and if snow was dangerous. He had never seen anything below 73°F (23°C) in his life. But he also hadn't seen anything hotter than 104°F (40°C).

In my life, though, I have experienced much higher temperatures than in Guiana or Suriname. In the Saudi Arabian desert for example. Many years ago I worked for the German-Saudi Liaison Office for Economic Affairs in Riyadh. I remember one weekend a colleague and I made a trip to Rubh Al-Khali, the "empty quarter", one of the driest and hottest places in the world. The temperature gauge in our Toyota

Landcruiser showed impressive 126°F (53°C). Almost 180 degrees Fahrenheit warmer than back then in Russia. And the same here: a simple car breakdown would have been a lethal event. But I lived to tell the tale, neither Ford nor Toyota are so bad after all.

My daughter Ronja in Amazonia

The difference with the heat experience in the equatorial jungle is that in Saudi Arabia I was hardly exposed to the crazy 126°F. You got out of the climatized car to take a few photos and got back in. It's like opening the oven to check on the cake. You get some hot air in your face, think to yourself, "pheeww hot," and quickly close the hatch again. Of course I was bragging about my heroism. But if I am being honest I went from a climatized home into a climatized office driving a climatized car. I ate in a climatized restaurant and shopped in a climatized supermarket. 126°F was for others, Pakistani road workers for example, but not for us spoiled Europeans, considering ourselves superior for no logical reason.

Rubh al-Khali, the empty quarter

In contrast, in Suriname the heat exposure was permanent and omnipresent. The day temperatures were around 100°F (38°C) every day, no exceptions, no A/C nowhere, Restaurants are all outside.

There was absolutely no way to escape it. If we had a really cold night, temperatures got down to a minimum of 81°F (27°C), which was hardly enough to cool down the boat from the heat of the day. The humidity of 80-100% added to the experience and so did the river water with its +86°F (30°C).

It is amazing how adaptive the human body is. It adapts much faster than the human mind. So much faster! This is what they told us back in the day when I was in the German navy:

"Freezing or sweating starts in your mind."

I didn't believe it at the time but it is true.

"Think of some place warm, a tropical beach for example!," was the suggestion of our officers, what I thought was pure military sarcasm.

But all in all they were right. Back then, they had their own reason for telling us because they made us have the roll-call in the snow in summer uniforms because the winter uniforms were delayed. So instead of our winter uniforms we received a lengthy speech about our tough grandfathers in Stalingrad and how embarrassed they were seeing us shivering in ridiculous 28°F (-2°C). This stung so much worse than the freezing cold wind. And as we tensed our chin muscles to make our grandfathers proud, we completely forgot about the irony that it wasn't our doubtlessly tough grandfathers in their light summer shirts who won the battle of Stalingrad 54 years ago, but the Soviets in their warm winter uniforms.

And while we were enviously peering to the American frigate *USS Stark*, docked just behind us, where our allied fellow sailors, bundled up in arctic coats, disappeared inside the heated helicopter hangar for their roll-call, we could not stop laughing about our First Officer's stupid joke:

USS Stark

“Now look at them sissies,” his harsh voice sounded over the stern artillery deck of our proud destroyer *FGS Rommel*, “they may have the mightiest military in the world, but destroy their A/C and you’ll win the war!”

Destroyer FGS Rommel

And so, despite the freezing temperatures and the wind stinging our faces, it already got a little warmer. He was a good officer. Yes, it is true, freezing or sweating starts in our minds and hearts. And no, under no circumstances do I want to become soft but I must admit, I look forward to the life-friendly climate of the Caribbean. As the plane lands in Prague, raising snowflakes, I take a decision: next year I will sail to Greenland. Even if it is just to prove to myself:

I am not a sissy.

Mother Carey's Chicken

Being in Germany now, in my home country away from home, I feel like I am on a speed dating competition. I will be here for only two weeks and friends, family and business partners are fighting for a spot in my bursting schedule. I feel very flattered, however, I feel overwhelmed and homesick, too.

Everyone has a name for me. They call me "freak", "sailing nerd", "outlaw" or "Cap'n Maik" or just "pirate". And they bombard me with questions. One of them is if I see a lot of sea life. Mostly my first answer is disappointing:

Despite the unbelievable vastness of life in the oceans, out there on the water, most of the times we sailors see nothing. We can go days and days at the same heading covering more than 100 nautical miles per day and see nothing but water and the sky in a thousand shades of blue. Most of life we see is close to land. There will be sea turtles and fish and dolphins and all kinds of birds, but out in the ocean encounters with living creatures (besides flying fish) are rare.

When I feel the disappointment of the land people I continue... But when we have them, these rare encounters with the creatures of the blue, they are breathtaking and extremely emotional. Whales, turtles, petrels, as a man of the sea you immediately connect with them, as different from us as they may be. They are not hostile and they are not afraid. They accept that we share the same habitat and consider us part of the family. Most of them probably never met people, because sadly enough, often this is a lethal experience for them and few live to tell the story.

No soul, neither human nor animal

Sea mammals are special of course. There is an immediate and direct line of communication. They are very close to us humans. But then there also are storm-petrels, mostly small birds of the sea that spend more than 90% of their lives on and over the oceans. Only breeding takes them to remote islands. They are true heroes, out there during any weather, enduring, tough, and curious. When they spot Seefalke they circle her for hours, circling closer and wider, higher and lower wondering what funny thing that is floating on the water. Then they come closer and start to hover over the mast top, checking out if it is a safe place to rest. Petrels have very weak feet. They hardly ever use them. Every landing that is not on water is a risky mission. If they break their feet, they die. On the islands they breed they have organized "runways" guarded by „flight controllers". Amazing, huh?!

Loggerhead turtle gliding through the sea

But the top of the mast or the railing is a relatively safe place. They are in no hurry. They circle, do some fishing, return to check it out from a different angle, take another bite and come back again. They are perfect pilots, too. They can hover in less than a foot distance with the wind howling and the boat rocking. Every navy SAR helicopter pilot would envy them for their skills. Did you know they got their name from Saint Peter, who was said to walk over water? And eventually, it can be after following the boat for 100+ miles, they will take a decision and land. They will just sit there and wouldn't be impressed by the noise of the boat, its crew or even my boat dogs. And they may sit there for a whole night. Resting spots are rare on the ocean and who would turn down a free ride? It might be the last opportunity for a while.

Storm petrel keeping me company

When I sailed from Martinique to Dominican Republic with more than 26,000 ft of water underneath my keel, I caught myself talking to one. He sat on my stern solar panel and would listen to me patiently. From time to time he would nod his head or shit on my solar panel as an obvious sign of disagreement. And at sunrise he would spread his wings and fly but hang around to protect my course. I guess I *am* a bit of a freaky sailing nerd. But storm-petrels are not just birds! They are the souls of fellow sailors lost at sea. They are Mother Carey's Chicken, messengers sent by Virgin Mary to warn sailors of an upcoming storm. But they are also "oiseau du diable", birds of the devil, "water-witches" to collect Davy Jones' toll.

Eventually my feathered friend would disappear with no goodbye, as it is sailors' tradition. Relief. It wasn't my turn yet.

And then I look up into the eyes of my confused land friends who are struggling to decide if they should call the police or a doctor, regretting they ever asked the question. So we quickly change topic and I try to pretend I fit in. And I understand that they do not understand.

They never will.

A Part of me apart from Me

Powerful

As you may remember, I am in Germany at the moment. I left my boat in Cuba for two weeks to take care of some important business. Despite being here for a week already, I am still suffering from the blunt culture shock. It is just a few days ago that I met with my good friend Julia. We had dinner in a sweet little restaurant that had obviously just recently opened. If my memory does not trick me, I still remember that place as a flower shop but I stopped trying to keep up with all the changes in this city long ago. While we are having our starters, she asks me what I miss most when out at sea or living on a sailboat, her curious eyes hanging on my lips in excited anticipation of the secret that is about to be revealed.

As usual my quick reply is “Nothing!”. It is honest. Surprise is filling the air and the disappointment becomes unbearable. So I think a bit harder.

“Don’t you miss your friends or your family or a hot bath, a comfortable bed or at least your favorite restaurant?,” her hoarse voice breaking the silence in sheer disbelief.

My brains are running hot, desperately trying to think of someone or something I miss. But no, I don’t. But will she really understand? Wouldn’t she think of me as a cold-blooded, stone-hearted, inhuman asshole? So finally I say:

“I miss good German bread. Nobody can make bread as the Germans do and what they call bread in most countries is a disgrace to the very word.”

We both laugh and as we move to the main course we move to the next topic. Pheeeww...

Seefalke is my home

But my thoughts are already flying. A sailor's yarn has been part of our business for centuries. We tell so many delusional cock-and-bull stories I am sure there is a special place in hell for us. But if not to others at least I want to be honest to myself. Am I really such an insensitive asshole with a heart made of stone?

So I consult the Cambridge Dictionary that tells me that "to miss someone" means "to be sad that a person is not present". Am I sad that a person is not present? There are people I sure would be happy to be present (for a while), but am I sad they are not? Here in Germany, I am sad that *Seefalke* is not around. So according to the scholars of Cambridge, I miss her. According to my heart I miss her even more. I have been gone just a week and in exactly one more week I will be with her again. So no big deal, I would think. But I do miss her. Why is it that I miss *Seefalke* despite the very short time we have been apart, but I don't miss friends and loved ones whom I haven't seen in many months? Or Cap'n Jack and Scout, my former furry, four-legged crew: I was so sad to see them go, but I don't miss them now. When I recently realized this, I shocked myself, a direct hit by the stone that is supposed to be my heart. My good friend Jimmy from Alabama would say

"Don't be such a German!"

I don't think, though, that Germans are not capable of missing. Even we Germans have feelings sometimes. I guess. So what is it that can tie a man to a boat closer than to a friend? Or a woman? It is true, if a girl would try to compete with *Seefalke* for my love, I'd pity the girl and sail away.

I'd pity the girl and sail away

Seefalke and I are the perfect team. Taken apart from each other, *Seefalke* would just be a piece of worthless scrap metal, and I would be a helpless, pathetic land critter, both of us doomed to drown miserably. But together we merge to a proud and powerful unit. Together we can sail the oceans and see the world. Together we will withstand malicious storms and endless calms. Together we have the courage to overcome our fears and venture out into uncharted waters and foreign lands again and again and again... No woman will divide us, no earthly pleasures will corrupt us. We stand together and, when it will be our turn, we'll go down as one. It's her who makes the man a captain.

When I read what I just wrote I start to understand. We only miss what we feel is a part of us, and *Seefalke* has become a part of me. And I am sure she is missing me, too.

It's time to go home.

It's time to go home

The Magic of Arrivals

I just arrived back on my boat *Seefalke*. She is currently docked in Marina Gaviota in Varadero, Cuba and after two weeks of painful separation, the two of us are finally reunited again. I caress the womanly curves of her wheel tenderly; I know she feels how much I missed her.

When talking with friends on land, I am often asked what I love about life on board and at sea. Now I sit down in the cockpit after more than 14 hours of traveling, finally relaxing in the mild, starry night. I decided to light a Cuban cigar to celebrate my return. It is one of the lighter ones, "Romeo y Juliet". I lean back looking at the twinkling stars, take a deep drag and recall one of the most recent conversations. We are sitting in a cozy restaurant in downtown Halle (Saale), Germany with home-style cooking and our drinks just arrived.

"I love the sea. I love to sail. I love to explore foreign countries. I love to meet people" I explain to my friend and former colleague Frank, "But even more than all that, I love arrivals. And departures!"

"But arrivals are the best! You just can't have them without departures. Now close your eyes and imagine this. (Ehm, if you close your eyes, you can't read this, so don't close your eyes but still imagine this):

You have your passage carefully planned. You studied all available handbooks, charts and tables. You downloaded the newest weather forecast. You made sure your charts are up to date, the waypoints are set. The provisions are bunkered, you are good on water and fuel. The dinghy is stowed and secured. The cabin is secure, hatches are closed. The winds are great with the tide in your favor. Check. You are going through the departure checklist again. You know the passage ahead will be long and challenging and you don't want to miss a thing. You loved it here, but you feel your restless sailor soul is dragging you out to sea again towards new horizons and beyond. You make your final round on deck and through the cabins. David Bowie's "Space Oddity" plays in the background: 'Commencing countdown, engines on. Check ignition and may god's love be with you…' You feel a little like Major Tom. You just don't want to end like him. Lazy Jack bags are open, sails are ready to hoist. Check. Rig is ok. Nav lights are ok. Check. Check. Deck is clear. Cockpit is clear. Check. Check. Bilges are dry. Seawater filter is clear. Check. Check. Sea cocks are closed. Check. The batteries are charged. The navigational instruments booted. Check. Check. Then you report to yourself: Ship is ready to weigh anchor. One last glance at the sky and you start the engine, hit the 'up' button for the electrical windlass. Comfortingly, the familiar clack-clack-clack-clack lifts the heavy chain, coming up, rumbling over the windlass and disappearing in the anchor locker, leaving a trace of stinky mud and mussels on the foredeck. It takes some time for the 130 ft chain to come up. Finally, the anchor, a 66 lbs Bruce, comes out of the water, swinging steadily before it noisily settles in its bracket. Then BEEP-BEEP-BEEP breaks through the silence. You are alerted at first but then you realize it's just the anchor alarm that you forgot to turn off, triggered by the boat slowly drifting away from the programmed position. If you forgot that, what else might you have forgotten? You switch it off and you return back to the foredeck to secure the anchor for the passage while your boat continues to slowly drift aft. You put the motor in gear, heading out of the protected bay of your anchorage that was your home for the last two weeks. As the space allows, you turn the bow into the wind, hoist the mainsail, furl out the genoa and set course to your first waypoint. Motor off. Silence. Just the wind and the waves. Peace. Tranquility. Solitude. All synonyms for pure happiness."

I see Frank nodding dreamily, as if he was on board with me. He takes a sip of his beer and I continue...

"When you have rounded the last rocks and reached the open ocean you know, this will be your heading for a week. You trim the sails and the autopilot is doing its work, reliably, untiringly. Good fellow! You set AIS and radar alarms, just in case. When you head into the cabin you feel a little redundant, which makes you smile, because it will allow you to take your first nap. Being redundant is not a bad thing."

Frank interrupts me, all upset and agitated: "I was just made redundant. It is a bad thing! It is a very bad thing! I didn't like it too much. I have a new job now but being made redundant totally sucks!"

360 degrees of freedom

He slams his hand on the table, some beer spills. I feel ashamed. Yes, the land has different rules than the sea. I clean the table with my sleeve and after a short moment of silence, I continue:

"It will take three days until the rhythm of the sea routine finally kicks in where you and your boat are working like well aligned clockwork. You and your boat become one, literally moving along on the same wavelength. Nothing but water in your entire field of vision. 360 degrees of water. 360 degrees of endlessness. 360 degrees of freedom.

Everything falls off you. All the hassle of the world seems so unimportant and petty. Impeachments, oil prices, stock exchange crashes, Coronavirus, stress with your wife, nothing could be less important. Whereas on land you check the news and your social media accounts a hundred times a day, you realize that you survive well without them. Quite easily in fact. And you love it. For you the world stands still. You are right inside your comfort zone in this wormhole where time and space bypass the rushing rest of the world. The world keeps turning underneath you, but you are independently floating in space. You think to yourself, 'This crazy Einstein nerd was right after all.' Days go by, maybe weeks. It doesn't really matter. But then all of a sudden LAND, expected yet surprising. Spotting first land after a long passage is always a lifting moment, magical and deeply moving. First you think it's an illusion, a fata morgana. You only believe it when it is confirmed. Too often you have been tricked by a cloud formation or simply a stain on your binoculars.

Land or clouds?

Land? Land!!

You are longing for it and dreading it at the same time. Sheer ambivalence got you. You dread the hassle when you get to land, clearing in, how to get cash and cell service, how many emails will be waiting for you, what else do you need to catch up with, etc... But you also envision a cool drink, a juicy steak and a close dance with a pretty girl. It doesn't take much to make a sailor happy after landfall."

This seems to have an effect on Frank. He suggests:

"Let's order some food, will we?! I'm getting hungry. They are supposed to have excellent steaks here."

The waitress takes our order but apologizes that the steaks are going to take about an hour today, as the restaurant is full and the kitchen busy. We are a little disappointed, but we order steaks anyway.

"Landlubbers cannot imagine how long it can take to actually make it to a harbor after you first spotted land on the horizon. Now assume the mountains at your destination are more than 3,000 ft high, clear skies provided, you will see them crawling over the horizon at a distance of approximately 60 nautical miles and at a speed let's say of five knots it will still take you twelve hours to arrive at the approach channel. Twelve very long hours."

The hour we have to wait for our steaks all of a sudden doesn't seem too long after all.

"Approaching land has visible signs. The first land-based birds arrive, the water is changing its color, while waves slowly and almost imperceptibly change their shapes and their frequencies. Almost intangibly the land is growing out of the horizon. Higher and higher but endlessly slow. You discover new details every time you check on it with your binoculars. First individual mountains, then forests and fields, later individual trees and buildings and eventually the shoreline. Then cars, people and life. You can smell the city, barbecue, car exhaust, eventually even the penetrant smell of sunscreen from the beach.

Thousand shades of blue

During the last week on the open ocean you saw one container ship in five days. Here, the sea is swarming with small fishing boats, freighters at anchorage or approaching the harbor, pilot boats going back and forth. You even see other sailboats. Where have they been all the time? Immediately all of them require your undivided attention. Then, finally, the approach buoy, you turn into the channel, following it past shoals and reefs, islets and rocks. Whereas further out the approach experience was like a still, like an image with no noticeable movements, now it is more like a movie, with sound even. Seagulls are screaming, waves are smacking against the rocks, the roaring motor of a speed boat is drowning out everything else for a moment until the deep triple *tooooot* of a huge cruise ship leaving its dock is letting everyone know her engines are in astern propulsion.

Lilliput in Wonderland

You pass endless piers and huge docks, you feel like a Lilliputian among all those giant ships and structures, like Lilliputian and Alice in Wonderland at the same time. You call the marina on VHF. They give you instructions how and where to dock: Med-mooring, stern in. You prepare fenders and lines as you squeeze into the narrow entry. Wedged in between an array of giants, the marina seems even tinier.

Final stretch

One more time tension comes up as you back into your assigned slip. Whereas it was calm during the approach, sudden gusts make your docking maneuver the last challenge of this passage. You remember Rocky's famous quote 'It's not over until it's over.' as you throw the lines to the helpful dockmaster who is waiting for you on the pier.

It's not over until it's over

When the boat is secured you jump on the pier to shake his hands. From the first moment you feel warm and welcome. This first moment is so important. It decides if you will like this place or not. Then you switch off the motor, make your last logbook entry, switch off the instruments, stow away the binoculars and put covers on the sails. You check the lines and fenders one more time before you grab your documents and head out to clear in. The pier is still rocking under your feet, but you know:

You made it.

Part Three:

Pandemics and Hurricanes

Back in Cuba

After two weeks in the fatherland I finally made it back to Varadero, Cuba and my boat that by now has become more home to me than anything else. For some reason I never planned to come to Cuba, but very often the unplanned experience turns out to be the most beautiful. I stayed in Cuba for almost three months, first in Varadero, later in Havana. I made a lot of friends and got to know the good, the bad, and the ugly face of Cuba.

But I will always remember Cuba as the country of Sunshine, Salsa and Socialism.

Sunshine, Salsa, Socialism

"Hey Maik!"

Somebody is shouting my name and abruptly I turn around. I see a pink Chevrolet '55 convertible taxi, and I see a woman, wearing an elegant long dress and a hat that makes every sombrero look tiny. Huge sunglasses cover what is left to see on her face. The sun is burning relentlessly. I squint. I see the elegant woman, the taxi with its driver and the bored security guard leaning against the gate. Nobody else is in my field of vision, but I don't see anyone who could possibly know my name or would have a reason to shout it. As the woman waves at me like greeting a good friend, I finally figure it must be her who called my name. So, I set off walking toward her. Is this Britta? Although she shares the same year of birth as the Cuban revolution, she looks much fresher. Britta had contacted me a week ago on Facebook. She had booked a flight to Varadero to go sailing with friends. They cancelled on her for a medical emergency, but the flight was booked, and she was not ready to give up on Cuba yet. Then she saw my post, saw that I am a sailor and I am in Varadero, and reached out to me. I had no plans and a free stern cabin. So, we had a deal.

A day later we were sitting in the Cubacar office to get our rental car for some inland exploration. Cubacar is the state-owned rental car company in Cuba.

"Don't wait until you run out of gas," is the clear warning when I am handed the keys, "you may not be able to come back."

So, we stop at the first gas station in Varadero and fill up the tank. I knew that gas stations in tourist areas get preferred deliveries. Now we are good to go. On the way to Havana we pass a huge oil field near Santa Cruz del Norte. I read that Cuba produces around 50,000 barrels every day. That's quite a figure, however not enough by far to cover its consumption of 150,000 barrels, leaving Cuba with a deficit of 100,000 barrels per day. A bad thing with their mighty neighbor trying to choke this socialist country off its lifelines. No wonder the battle cry of the local soccer team, written in huge red letters on the stadium wall, is 'Socialismo o Muerte!' (Socialism or death).

When we arrive in Havana an hour later, we drop off our luggage at our AirBnB place. Rossana, our sweet host, asks us if she should prepare us dinner and we quickly agree. Then she asks the question, that I am sure she will regret for the rest of the day:

"What would you guys like to eat?"

We have heard so much about Ropa Vieja, Cuba's national beef dish, so we asked her if she could prepare it for us for dinner. She hesitates a split second, but she agrees, and we head out into the city center. The architecture is stunning, the atmosphere friendly, the weather wonderful, tourists aplenty. The afternoon passes in a heartbeat. At least for us. When we later eat delicious Ropa Vieja with Rossana she is overly happy. She simply cannot stop smiling. When we ask her for the reason for her happiness, she says she is so happy she could hunt down some beef today. After the economic crisis in the 90's, cattle farming in Cuba dropped tremendously. It is less than a third today of what it used to be. As the black market for beef and dairy products flourished, the government invented intense control mechanisms for beef and dairy production and draconic punishments for illegal beef production and sales. In fact, so draconic it scared almost everyone away from this industry altogether. As a result, beef is scarce and expensive, the opposite of the doubtlessly good intentions of the government.

Rossana's daughter later tells me she traveled one hour to a specific supermarket that supposedly had beef today and waited in line for two more hours to get let in. I feel bad for having asked for Ropa Vieja. I had no idea. I understand now it is like asking for fresh lobster in my hometown in central Germany. With full bellies and feeling a little ashamed, we go to sleep. I decide to wait and take a shower the next morning. Another miscalculation as I'm about to find out.

We wake early because today we want to go to Viñales. Viñales in the western mountains is famous for its tobacco and coffee plantations. It's about a 2.5-hour drive. When I try to take a shower, very little water comes out of the faucet. A few drops, that's it. At breakfast we learn that water is shut off over night to reduce energy and water consumption. Only tourist regions are excluded. That is usual. Unusual, however, is that this morning the gas is also shut off. A quick call to her mother who lives on the other end of town tells Rossana that the whole city is affected. But it wouldn't be Cuba if there wasn't a solution to every problem. Their neighbor has an electrical stove, and he is happy to make coffee for us and heat up the milk. Mhhhhh, real cow's milk! Pure luxury! Cuba may be the only country in the world, where coffee often is cheaper than milk.

When we get in the car the warning of the rental car guy echoes in my head... "Don't wait until you run out of gas or you may not come back!". The tank is half-empty, so I think it's a good time to top up. When I stop at the first gas station, they just shake their heads. The second has a line too long for my spoiled western taste. The third one has no line, but also no gas. Eventually, and slightly frustrated, I return to the gas station with the long line and do what they do here, I humbly line up. Because they have what I want and there is no other way to get it. But if you think waiting is wasted time, you're wrong. I love my job as a travel writer. What for most others may be wasted time for me is the perfect opportunity to learn more about people's lives and why exactly fuel is scarce in this country. We already know Cuba produces only a third of its consumption and both the continued chaos in their brother state Venezuela, Cuba's No. 1 oil supplier and the US embargo has hit them hard. Whatever is available goes into tourism and military first, then state owned transport. Little is left for private transportation.

No line – no gas

An hour later and with a full tank we venture out of Havana onto the motorway and west. The quality of the road is ok, traffic is low. Hardly any cars but lots of horse coaches. Yes, you heard right, horse coaches on a four-lane motorway. Smart, the fuel they use is fairly abundant. About two thirds of the way there we pass an accident. A car hit a bus. How they managed to meet each other on the empty roads will remain their secret forever. We get flagged down and we are asked if we can take Javier to Viñales so he can come back with a spare bus to pick up his colleagues. We know it's not a trick. Hitchhiking in Cuba is a form of public transport and it is absolutely safe. Javier works for the national park in Viñales and during the remaining hour of our drive we learn a lot about Viñales and the province Pinar del Rio. We learn that the soil is red and full of minerals. We learn the cool nights and the sunny days in the mountains are best for coffee and tobacco. We learn that the city Pinar del Rio is the tobacco capital of Cuba.

Tobacco fields in Pinar del Rio

As we arrive in Viñales we drop off Javier at the tobacco farm, and he arranges a free tour for us and a cigar roll course in return for the ride. Cigar production is all about leaves: shade leaves and sun leaves and upper leaves and lower leaves and wet leaves and dry leaves and cover leaves and...

Cigar rolling lesson under Che's critical supervision

Anyway, the only thing I remember is that Che used to dip his cigars in honey. No wonder he always had one in his mouth. Imagine if El Comandante would have just sucked a honey spoon instead! Would have looked silly for a revolutionist, wouldn't it?!

We were hoping to see the ecological coffee plantation, too. No cars go there and walking is pretty far. Horses are the only mode of transport. Cargo is carried on oxcarts. It's been a while since I last rode a horse. But hey, it's like riding a bicycle, you never unlearn it, right?! Britta and I exchange some looks waiting for the other to bail out, but the battle of will ends in a clear stalemate and off we go, at first moving at a slow pace but later we get braver and gallop the last miles through the valley and past tobacco fields. You only live once, right?! And I'd rather that life be short than boring!

Our ride

On the coffee plantation they grow Arabica and Robusta in certified ecological cultivation. We learn the difference, that I forgot again and that they mix 80% Arabica and 20% Robusta for their local produce. We taste some coffee and honey from coffee flowers. Oh my, that is delicious! I understand why all school kids want to be like Che, they all love honey as he did. ("Seremos como el Che" – "We will be like Che" is the motto of the Cuban Pioneers.)

I take a pass on the local rum and have another coffee instead. The waitress is cute, too. She tells us that they only produce four tons of coffee per year on this ecological farm where everything is done by hand. At the end we even make everybody join us in singing the 'pilón', the song they sing while grinding the beans.

Coffee plantation

My crotch is still sore from the way here, but we cannot stay forever. The coffee girl is sweet, but I am not meant to end up as a coffee farmer in Cuba. It's just not my destiny, sorry, girl! So, I saddle my horse (it is already saddled but it sounds better) and spur it into the sunset, with Britta right behind me. It is so much fun but as I crawl off my stallion, I have the strong feeling the ride put an abrupt end to any reproductive ambitions I still might have had.

I understand now why lonesome cowboys remain lonesome.

Heavy transport

After we return our four-legged transport we go to the farmers' restaurant Javier recommended. They had expected us, and the food is fantastic, but hell, is the chief waiter curious. By the time we finish our main course he knows more of Britta and me than I knew about my wife when I married her. By the time we finish our dessert, I am wondering what the Cuban state security would make of all the made-up bullshit stories we told him. Maybe I will end up on a coffee plantation after all. In chains, learning my lessons.

One more reason to seize the day and dance as if there was no tomorrow. The opportunity is good as they have their weekly street festival. The main street is already blocked, and bars and restaurants have moved their tables out. Live music is playing and old and young are rhythmically moving their hips to the salsa tunes. The air is full of laughter and love and happiness. Life is beautiful!

Adhoc street festival

Less beautiful is the long ride back to Havana during the pitch-black night. We arrive only when the first light glows over the horizon. Another day is waiting for us. Another day in beautiful Cuba. I am sure it will be full of sunshine, salsa and socialism again.

Mexico on the Verge of Covid

As much as I loved Cuba, eventually the scarcity of almost everything got on my nerves. Obviously, despite all my perceived indifference towards privation, I need to concede that I am still just a spoiled Western post-war kid of capitalism and abundance. I can go a year without a hot shower and with just one pair of shoes but a few weeks without fresh milk and a juicy steak put me on my last legs. So after three months of time travel I set sail back to the future, to Mexico.

Whereas the passage from Havana to Isla Mujeres was short and uneventful, the world stopped to be as we knew it on the other side.

Life under the Yellow Flag

My vessel is healthy, and I request free pratique

"Open – Rain or Shine", the neon sign over the entrance to Skull's Landing invites its guests. It is one of those signs that normally can be switched from "open" to "closed" just this one doesn't have a "closed" option. A great marketing move. Skull's Landing is the local cruisers' hangout with Happy Hour from 1400hrs to 1900hrs.

Skull's Landing in Isla Mujeres

There are two things in life that are certain: 1) At one point you will die. 2) Sailors cannot resist Happy Hours. Happy Hour at Skull's Landing means half price drinks and live music, a combination providing fertile yarning grounds. This is where heroes are born, sea monsters are fed and Neptune is worshipped. But now is the Fasting Period, not only for religious Christians but also for us heathenish seafarers, because Neptune's local temple remains closed, rain or shine. Corona is out in the worst possible double meaning of the term.

When I left Cuba exactly three weeks ago, I remember I couldn't understand the immigration officer when she asked me the simplest questions. That could have been due to my poor Spanish or due to the mask she was wearing or both. Other than that in Cuba was still business as usual whereas the rest of the world already started to go nuts. When I arrive at Isla Mujeres in Mexico the clearance procedures are delayed as the officials are waiting for instructions from the top. However, I am able to clear in without any further problems. But let me give you a short idea of what „without any further problems" means:

Whale sharks are Isla Mujeres mascot

First I have to get a total of five physical copies of each of the following documents: the boat registration, the crew's passports, the Zarpe (clearance documents of the previous port) and the crew list, stamped by the previous ports authority.

With these copies I first check in at the Port Captain's office that, in Mexico, is a department of the navy. He is responsible for all boat traffic in his jurisdiction, national as well as foreign. Then I have to wait for the immigration doctor. He is a nice guy with the body of a well fed sumo wrestler and arrives in an outfit that I believe he stole from the movie 'Outbreak'. I don't blame him. If anyone is exposed to evil viruses it is him. After a short medical examination which basically consists of the measurement of my body temperature, a deep look into my eyes and a few medical questions I get my 'Declaración Maritime de Sanitad'. I know I better hold on to it tightly because I will need it further down in the process.

Next I am sent to immigration. The immigration office is a few blocks down the street and the girls there are welcoming and sweet. They give me a few forms to fill and then send me to the bank to pay the immigration fee. When I return with my receipt (which easily can take an hour or longer) I am issued an immigration card that gives me (European, US, Canadian and many other citizens) a 180 day status. (Hold on to it tightly, too. Don't lose it. Also keep the receipt of the immigration fee. It is the ticket to the next ride.)

Back at the Port Captain's office I present the rewards I earned in the previous steps of the quest and patiently wait for the customs and veterinarian officers to arrive. They come with more forms and more stamps. Make sure that all five copies you made of all the earlier documents have those stamps or you will be screwed later. After that I go back to the bank to pay the customs processing fee and return to the Port Captain's office with the receipt.

After all this is done, I turn all this in to the Port Captain's office to have him issue my 'Autorización de Arribo'. But if you think I am done now (all this takes an entire day) you are wrong. If you want to stay longer than five days you have to apply for a temporary import permit (TIP) for your boat. This is done by the customs department located in the Port Captain's office of Cancun on the mainland. You need to have an appointment, though, which I learn the hard way when I first show up without one.

There I need 60 USD in cash, all the documents I received from the Port Captain with five (!) stamps on each and an official document, preferably the boat registration with the engine number of my boat. (If your boat registration does not show the engine number, you have to make a photo of the nameplate and write a letter in Spanish in which the owner confirms that this engine is on his boat.) Then I am issued the temporary import permit which is valid for ten years.

Anyway, after three days my boat is a paper load of documents heavier and now has the privilege of being legally cleared into the United States of Mexico.

Seefalke is granted free pratique in Mexico

Isla Mujeres before

Isla Mujeres after

Still at this time there is business as usual on the island. The beaches are populated by Mexican and foreign tourists, the bars and restaurants are packed and the streets full of life. The island of the blissful, whereas the rest of the world is drowning in curfews and lockdowns. But at one point it is clear that not even the Mexicans could dodge this development forever. Soon I take the decision to stay there until the whole chaos is over, delaying my plans to head South to Belize, Guatemala, Honduras and Costa Rica and out of the hurricane belt. My hope is that the big blast is over before the hurricanes are starting to make this part of the world uncomfortable. And if not, my plan B is to stay here until I see a hurricane coming over the Atlantic. It would only take me a week of sailing to get out of the hurricane belt. And if I had to I would anchor out, wherever that would be and continue my quarantine further South. So quietly I started to stock up my provisions to be prepared.

The first noticeable sign of increased strain is the suspension of alcohol sales. Bars and restaurants are still open and tourists are still coming and going. At this point also more tourists start going than coming and the island gets noticeably emptier. About a week later all restaurants and bars are closed and only essential stores are allowed to open. However, our freedom is not limited in any way, we can still go to the beach, go snorkeling and go shopping in the supermarkets. I start to go to the supermarket every day and buy just a little more each day than I would use to stock up my provisions. You never know after all.

The tensions are high and the nerves are blank. I once meet Capi, the immigration doctor on his heavily overloaded scooter. He immediately recognizes me and stops. He is very upset, so I try to calm him down but he is not very receptive to my jokes. He is looking for the crew of a French boat that arrived late the day before. The coast guard had visited their boat but nobody was on board. Now they are searching the whole island for them to put them back on board for their 14 days quarantine. This is also the time when tourists who arrive by ferry from the mainland are turned back on the same ferry they arrive on. Whereas a week earlier the streets were populated by lightly-dressed tourists they are now patrolled by heavily armed marines and police pick-up trucks making loudspeaker announcements. The national disaster response service (Protección Civil) would politely but firmly ask people to leave the beach and return to their homes.

Today, as the new orders of the Port Captain arrive, I am stocked as though I am about to embark on a nonstop circumnavigation. We are now only allowed to go to land using the dinghy dock of the Port Captain. Only one person per boat is allowed to go to land and only after prior approval by the Port Captain. At the dinghy dock this person needs to check in with the soldier on duty there and has a maximum of 1.5 hours to go shopping in designated stores. New arrivals are ordered to keep a 14 day strict quarantine.

Through our local cruisers' net we keep the communication channel to the Port Captain and he is very helpful and understanding of our needs. So he has arranged water bottle trucks to come to the pier and trash trucks to pick up our trash, a spell of luxury these days.

Any type of touristic activity is now prohibited. No surfing, no snorkeling, no kayaking... I think this is fair and helps to not turn the locals against us. If they all need to stay at home and cannot use the beach and see us foreigners having a blast, that wouldn't be good. Not at all. So yes, I hate it but I support it. Whereas I hear of similar rules and restrictions throughout the Caribbean, generally, the moods are high and who, if not we bluewater sailors, is prepared for this? I have daily contact with friends throughout the Caribbean. Whatever there is on the news about poor sailors in need stuck in the Caribbean, I cannot confirm. I can also not confirm that sailors in need are being sent back to sea without provisions and water. I can imagine there are a few singular cases of local personnel overreacting but in general, what I see is a strict but very understanding application of the necessary quarantine rules. An unpredicted change of plans is no emergency. We sailors tend to change plans more often than our underwear anyway.

I have no idea where all this is headed but I am sure at one point Skull's Landing will be able to put on their sign again „Open – Rain or Shine".

Family Reunification

Some time ago I took the difficult decision to leave friends and family behind and live my dream at sea. As you may have seen, till now it is not only sunshine and rainbows, it is a life full of sacrifice and privation, for me it's absolutely worth it, though. Whereas it is hard at times to have my family spread over different continents, during a global pandemic it becomes cruel. My daughter is with her mother in Germany, hence in relative safety, but my seventeen-year-old son goes to college in Mobile, Alabama. They just shut down his college and his dorm, basically putting him on the street. Resourceful as he is, he easily found a place to stay with friends in Texas but for me as a parent in this unclear situation, that was unsatisfactory. I wanted to have him close when the shit hit the fan and also I did not want his friends to have the burden of responsibility in these uncertain times. So I booked him a flight to Mexico, not knowing that this was the last day flights would go for a long time.

But the adventure had just begun.

Father and son

Call of Duty

It is dark. Pitch black. Impervious. Only scattered low declination stars hint at the existence of more boats at this anchorage. I know there are dozens.

Most of them have their anchor lights on, but not all of them. During the day I spent some time memorizing a path through this maze of boats and shoals, set umpteen waypoints on my GPS, in case I had to leave my anchorage at night. Until the last moment I hoped it would not become necessary. Hope dies last. It just did its last breath for me.

My hope died with a phone call of an unknown Mexican number at 0100hrs in the morning:

"Papa, my phone is dead." I hear Tom's voice mixed with static. "I don't have enough money, my debit card doesn't work. I am using the phone of a taxi driver at Cancun airport. I am negotiating with him. I think I can convince him to drive me to our meeting point."

And then the line is dead. As dead as my hope. This was the first time I heard from Tom, my 17-year old son, after that mysterious text message I received in the late afternoon:

"I arrived in Mexico-City. I got released after I got arrested at the security checkpoint. They didn't like my keychain. All good now. Headed to gate."

Everyone who knows me knows that my nerves could easily replace Golden Gate Bridge's steel cables. But I must admit that this text message put some additional strain on them. Just very shortly though, until I benevolently weighed the information contained in this message:

Firstly, he arrived in Mexico-City. As the name indicates this place is in Mexico. So, he made it across the border of which I didn't exactly know if it was still open. In the previous evening they said that the Mexican border to the US would be closed from midnight on for "non-essential" travel. Is a minor re-uniting with his father "essential"? It sounded like it. So the first part made me relieved.

Secondly, he got released. This means he is not arrested anymore, so I don't have to bail him out of a Mexican jail. Wonderful! This has the potential to make my day.

Then the worrying part, he got arrested for his keychain. I remember that stupid key chain. It is a live .300 AAC Blackout 7.62 mm round made inoperative and turned into a souvenir. These rounds are only used by special forces or – by my son. I got it for him a few years ago when I took him to a shooting range in Birmingham, AL. Don't judge me! And yes, it is a bad idea to take a live round onto an airplane, even an inoperative one. For a short moment I wondered why this hadn't already become a problem when he boarded that flight to Mexico-City. But then it occurred to me that he flew from Texas. No more questions.

Finally, and last but not least he was headed to his gate which means there was a chance he would still make his connection to Cancun. As he said, all was good after all and so I relaxed. The rest of the afternoon I spend watching this little airplane icon on my Flightradar24 app almost unnoticeably creeping towards Cancun. And when I am not watching that little icon, I am studying Google Earth.

On my screen I am going over the coastline of Cancun again and again. Zooming in, then zooming out, scrolling further North, then zooming in again. Then repeating the same procedure further South. I feel like in the Combat Information Center of a naval landing ship, masterminding a D-Day like satellite aided naval landing operation. I have to find a beach where I could land my dinghy at a place that had access to the public and was in reasonable walking distance to our meeting point. I am happy now that we agreed on a fallback position before. Something had told me that we might need that, knowing that Tom is notoriously out of money and his phone notoriously out of battery.

Our fallback position is in the front of the ferry terminal at Puerto Juarez. This is where the ferries go from Cancun to Isla Mujeres, my current anchorage. A short 20 minutes ride with those high speed ferries. Just they don't go from midnight to 0630hrs in the morning. For a split second I consider just telling him to cuddle up with his clothes on a beach and wait for the first morning ferry. I reject this option as soon as I imagined what his mother would do to me if she found out. I feel the anticipated pain and make *Seefalke* ready for some nighttime evac ops.

So, I can't land at the ferry terminal. That is obvious. The North is no option, either. When I went to Cancun to receive my temporary import permit I noticed that the northern beach section was part of a military facility. I figure conducting a night landing operation exercise at a military facility might be taken the wrong way and would possibly cause more trouble than a keychain. So I look at the beaches further south, where there seemed to be mainly hotels. I have seen the hotels in this area, they all have private beaches to protect their valuable guests from us trespassers. Like in my favorite computer game "Call of Duty" when you have to decide between assault or stealth strategy I evaluate my chances. The military facility is the professional level. I hadn't played the game in a while and don't feel ready for that just yet. At the hotels I have to evade a few surveillance cameras for sure, avoid the guards and jump a fence or a wall and do the same in reverse order when I would come back again. That still sounds pretty advanced to me. There has to be something for beginners, too! But hey, isn't there a place with beached boats? I zoom in a little more. Yes, there is a pier with fishing vessels and a short beach section with small fishing boats. That looks good! Really good! This means that spot was good for beaching with no reefs and had access to the public. And for fishermen nighttime is nothing special. They wouldn't be surprised to see a boat arriving at night and call the police on me. Also this beach section is maximum a one kilometer walk from our rendezvous location. Perfect. Rookie-level. I mark this beach position in my Navionics system and chart my route.

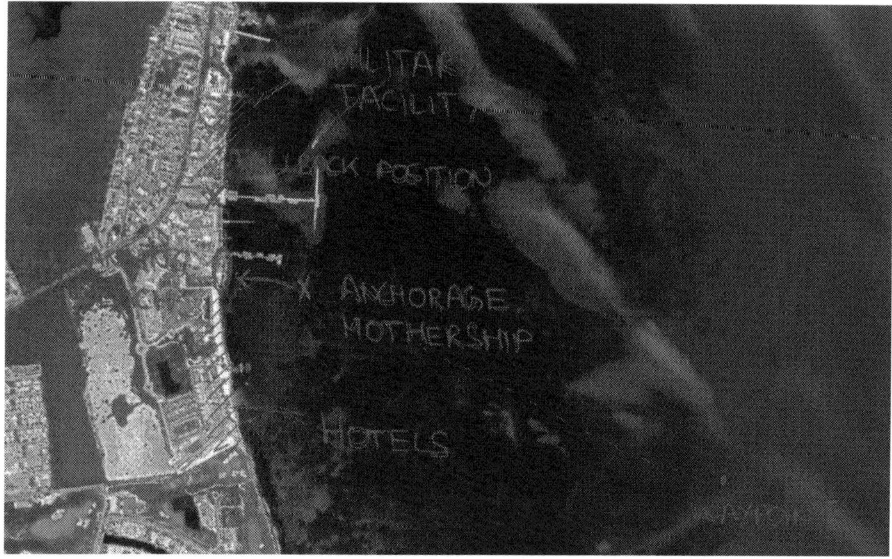

Call of Duty game map

The next challenge is the weather. Force five winds from the East are in the forecast. This means I will have to anchor *Seefalke* off a lee shore with onshore wind and most probably I will have to deal with some surf on the beach. Great! Not impossible but it's gonna get wet!

So after the phone call I crank the 62 hp Vetus Diesel, turn on the deck light that brightly illuminates the foredeck and unlock the anchor. Clack-clack-clack-clack the chain rattles over the windlass and into the chain locker. From time to time I stop for a few seconds to allow the boat to move forward towards the anchor and take the strain out of the chain. After a few minutes the boat is right on top of the anchor. I mark the position on my GPS, put the engine into gear and thread my way out of the anchorage and into the channel. The channel leads me close past the ferry terminal on Isla Mujeres and past Playa Centro. The beach that never sleeps does sleep after all. Ok, it is 0130hrs. At 0130hrs every beach should have the right to sleep, and every man, too, fathers excluded I guess. I yawn. Finally I round the two markers with the red three second flash identifiers and take a turn to port onto my course for Cancun. With the nasty current in Bahia Mujeres, which in fact is rather a channel than a bay, it is going to take me 1.5 hours. I know I will make it up on the way back.

As I am leaving the lee of Isla Mujeres I feel how the seas are building up. Nothing serious for *Seefalke* but mentally I am already in my dinghy trying to make it to the beach half-way dry. The night is clear, it is a spectacular sight, only slightly light-polluted by the illuminated skyline of Cancun. Falling stars are guiding me, the autopilot keeps us on a straight line to our next waypoint. I love it. No ship out here. The marine version of social distancing maybe, I think with a bitter smile, my thoughts inevitably circle around the all dominating news item, with a late night sailor-minded touch of course.

Corona has the world by its balls, this is certain. The world doesn't like it but the more the world is trying to shake it off, the harder the squeeze. When I left Cuba a little over a week ago, the world in the Caribbean was still ok. When I arrived in Mexico after a three day passage, nothing remained as we know it. Mexico was almost the only country in the entire Caribbean that would still allow arrivals without quarantine. Everybody else had closed their sea borders. At the moment no ship is fast enough to beat the current development. In the meantime, Cuba started to expel all 60,000 tourists, Europe was in an entire lockdown with strict curfews and the US shut down colleges and schools and entire states. This was when Tom became homeless. He usually lives at a dormitory at the University of South Alabama in Mobile but then moved to friends in Texas. As much as I appreciated their hospitality (Thank you, Dale!!) I wanted Tom close if and when the shit hits the fan, and there was way too much shit populating the airspace around way too many fans to take my chances. So I put him on a plane from Dallas to Mexico-City, apparently at the very last moment. One day later the flight connection was suspended.

Shortly before 0300hrs I reach my waypoint and zig-zag through the numerous shoals. All sand here and with *Seefalke's* hull made from solid marine steel I am not really worried about touching the ground. Everything looks slightly different in the dark reality than it did on the high res satellite images on my screen. But I can see the ferry terminal with its parked ferries. I can see the pier with the fishing trawlers and I can see the hotels further South. And there I see the beach. Or better I know it's there because I don't see a thing. It is the only section of the coastline that is dark. I check the beach with my Steiner binocular. A great piece! I see maybe one dozen beached small fishing boats, all beached and anchored with a stern anchor. I see a little gap between two boats that I decide to aim for. I also see a dark undefined structure that possibly could be a wooden dock reaching out into the sea. But I am not sure. If it is, I will dock my dinghy there. Would be much easier than beaching in this uncomfortable surf.

Landing craft ready to launch

When I have around 2 ft water below my keel I feel it is a good time to drop the anchor. I set 100 ft of chain in 7 ft of water. I drive it in real good, too, revving up the Vetus in reverse. That should be enough, even on a lee shore with this swell. I turn on every light I have to illuminate *Seefalke* as much as I can. I want to minimize the chance that a drunk fisherman drives his boat right into it because he is going by memory and not by sight. Then I take my Steiner and step into the dinghy, my tiny rubber landing craft. The dinghy is full of water, partly because of the waves, partly because it has a leak, so I start bailing. At least the motor cranks on the first pull. The Cubans who fixed it back at the boatyard in Varadero did a fantastic job. So, I put the little 2.5 Mercury in gear and head for what has become Omaha Beach to me. As I come closer I almost bump into a fishing boat anchored with no lights on but I manage to dart sideways at the last moment. The surf is rocking me badly, it is almost impossible to control my tiny boat with its toy as a motor. A rodeo is kindergarten against this.

Then an abrupt stop. Huh? Did I hit the ground? No, I didn't. The motor got caught by an anchor-rode that I didn't see. I am lucky it didn't rip the motor off the transom, or myself. As I untangle the rode I can now identify that black structure that I saw from *Seefalke*. It really is a small wooden dock, reaching into the sea just enough so that I don't need to lift the motor. Perfect. I tie the dinghy to one of the poles and jump on land. I can see streetlights in the distance and the lights of a supermarket so yes, as I thought from Google Earth, there is public access. I trudge through the sand with my heavy military boots and head to the ferry terminal. But Tom is not there. To be precise nobody is there. Nobody and nothing. The street is deserted, not a single soul, not a single car. I call him, shout his name again and again. The only response is coming from some huge stray dogs barking back at me. Hush, puppies… But no Tom.

Finally I decide to go into the terminal. And there I see him. He had already made friends with the security guys there and had persuaded the owner of the little store to let him charge his mobile phone. Yeah, he doesn't waste a minute to socialize, even in times of social distancing. A handshake, a hug and we walk back to the beach together. At the beach we run into a fisherman, in my basic Spanish I explain to him that we used his dock temporarily to get back to our sailboat. He looks at me with big eyes and even greater pupils and has no further questions but he watches every step we take with amused interest. I think he is just high as a kite and thinks that he best not mess with those organized traffickers. Because this is how we must look to him: A ship anchors in the night, one man without bags comes ashore, two men with bags leave the shore, no words spoken, the ship disappears into the dark, he sure doesn't want to mess up this delivery.

The dinghy is too small for the two of us and Tom's luggage. So we first load his bag and his backpack. Then I push the dinghy over the surf and all the way out where our mothership is patiently waiting in the dark. Then I go back for Tom.

The mothership is waiting in the dark

Wet from tip to toe I crank the engine and weigh the anchor and under the monotonous sound of the powerful Diesel we disappear into the night. Then I call his mom. It is 0420hrs when I make the entry in the ship's log

"Tom retrieved. Mission complete. Headed back to Isla Mujeres."

At 0530hrs the anchor drops at the exact same spot where it was five hours ago. Finally we go to sleep as if nothing ever happened.

No big deal after all.

Island of the Blissfully Condemned

It felt good to finally have Tom onboard even though he had the feeling of getting kidnapped and deported. Yes, sometimes we parents have to take tough decisions. He felt locked down in paradise prison. He attended his classes remotely but he missed learning (and not only learning, I assume) with his friends, so for him, this lockdown, as for many people around the world, was not a pleasant experience.

However, we, the almost 50 boats in the Bahia of Isla Mujeres, got organized. And while the first orders of the Port Captain overshot the mark badly, we could discuss solutions with the Port Captain who turned out to be a reasonable man. So at the end, it was the Isla Mujeres Cruisers Net's achievement that the cruisers' conditions during the lockdown were as comfortable as they could possibly be.

Hailing Channel 13

Isla Mujeres Anchorage

"Good morning, this is Isla Mujeres Cruisers Net. It is our purpose to stay connected, exchange information and build the community of cruisers. Your participation is encouraged.," at exactly 0800hrs the familiar voice greets all sailors currently anchored or docked at Isla Mujeres, Mexico.

The voice belongs to Lisa, who is our net controller today. She is from Canada and lives with her husband Ken on board their catamaran

S/V Minaki. Her voice has something soothing. Formal but friendly, clear but compassionate. It is the kind of voice you want to hear when you are in distress calling for help. Luckily none of the sailboats is in distress so the first question regarding medical and security emergencies remains unanswered.

"Nothing heard," Lisa wraps it up. It is one of the rare occasions this signal has a positive meaning and also puts a positive note to today's radio conference on VHF channel 13. What follows is some trivia about this day in history and local weather and tide information. When I first tuned in I thought that was a bit weird but later I understood it really builds the international community when we learn what happened on the same day in all our different countries.

The diversity becomes tangible when the channel is open for general check-ins.

"Good morning – *Cookie Monster*", "Bonjour – *Penelope*", "Bon giorno – *Shaula*", "Guten Morgen – *Seefalke*", "God morgon – *Chibidarra*", "Buenas dias – *Donna Dee*" the check-ins are coming in, the various accents only let you guess from which end of the world they found their way into Isla Mujeres.

Prisoners in paradise

Today's count is 42 boats. 42 crews from all over the world, sharing a cell in Corona jail.

Which is not too bad after all. The most common phrase you hear these days is "There are worse places to be stuck." It is true. We all agree on it. And the Isla Mujeres Cruisers Net is one of the reasons why.

While the radio conference moves on to new arrivals, my thoughts go to my friends in Mexico's Eastern neighbour Cuba, locals as well as sailors. Cuba has changed from the Island of the Blissful to the Island of the Damned within days. All ports and marinas are closed. Sailors in ports had to leave the ports and if they were lucky, they were allowed to anchor out. A nationwide curfew is applied, food is rationed, police with sticks are beating everyone who dares to set a foot on the street back home. Transport is shut down completely. The supermarkets there are not famous for their abundance in normal times already, I don't even want to imagine what they look like now, no wonder that sailors there are considering alternatives. I love Cuba, but it is not a good place to be stuck these days. Isla Mujeres is a great alternative. Of course our freedom is limited. We need to get clearance for every dinghy movement and touristic activities are prohibited. However, arrivals and departures are still being processed, shore visits are still permitted for essential business. Live and let live. This is also an achievement of our Cruisers Net.

Whereas at the beginning of the Mexican Corona countermeasures there was much chaos and everyone came with bits and pieces of information, it was the Isla Mujeres Cruisers Net that put together the mass of orders, rules and regulations for sailors like a mosaic. The complete picture revealed gaps and contradicting overlaps that could be addressed with one voice. Soon the Port Captain, in whose jurisdiction we fall discovered the benefit of using the Cruisers Net as an effective communication channel. Michelle and Steve from

S/V Pili Aloha quickly became our representatives and took on this exhausting yet thankless task. Much easier for the Port Captain to just talk to them rather than nailing the announcements to every tree on the ocean.

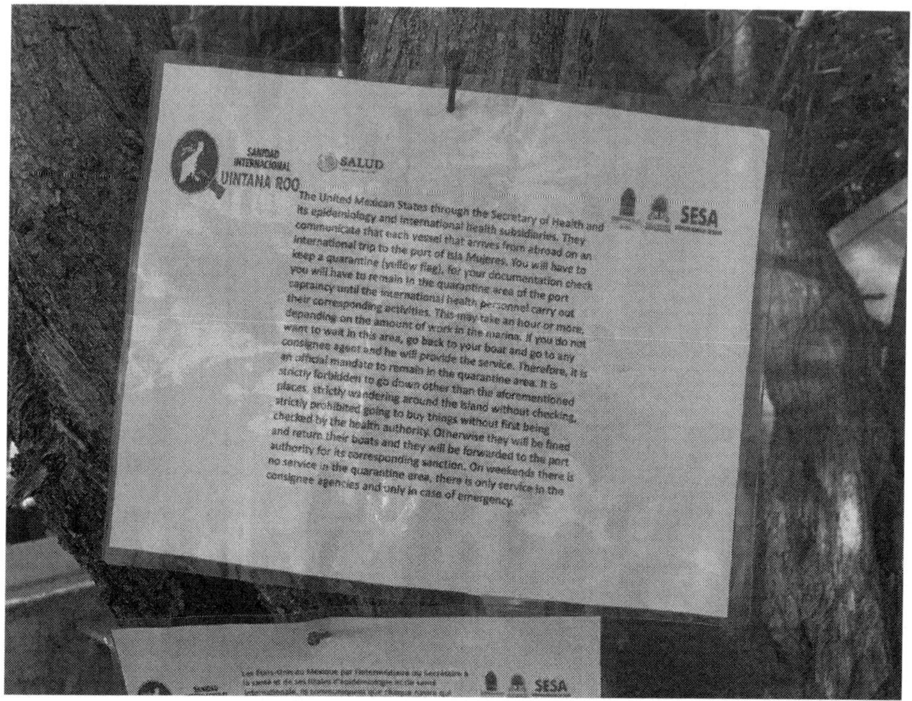

Port Captain's instruction nailed to a tree

While the restrictions got tougher and tougher the Isla Mujeres Cruisers Net first collected and then raised our concerns with the Port Captain who is very understanding and as accommodating as the situation allows. So trash collection was arranged as well as water delivery. He allows the use of the Port Captain's dock for shopping purposes and short day sails to dump black water into the ocean.

So it is not a big surprise that departures from Isla Mujeres are scarce and that part of the radio conference also ends with a "Nothing heard" from Lisa and we are moving on to "General Announcements".

Trash collection

"*Wind Magic*"

"*Wind Magic, go!,*" *Wind Magic* gets acknowledged to go ahead with the transmission.

Every morning, I am astonished all over again by the strict radio discipline in this group. As if everyone here is a trained navy radio operator.

"This is *Wind Magic*. Our yacht club opened its water hose for the general use of the cruisers. You can take your dinghy to the yacht club's dock and take as much water as you need. Please don't get off your dinghy and don't leave trash on the dock. Over."

"*Wind Magic* this is *Minaki*. Thank you for this generous offer."

Water delivery

"*Starship*"

"*Starship, go!*"

"This is *Starship*. We are currently producing masks for 100 Pesos each. Money will be donated to a local food bank. Orders will be taken after the net. Over."

"*Starship*, this is *Minaki*. A wonderful idea, thank you!"

The helpfulness is overwhelming. Mark from *Cockpit* offers to organize propane deliveries, *Polaris* will bring fresh fruits and vegetables to *Penelope* whose crew is still in their mandatory 14 day quarantine and Bram from *Donna Dee* offers a trash collection run.

As the conference moves on to "Boat Problems" I admit my thoughts drift off a bit. I have been solo sailing quite some time now but I have never felt lonely or lost. It is this wonderful community that makes you feel there is a solution to every problem. Sometimes there is even a solution when there is no problem. I remember, it must have been day two or three after my arrival, I was still unaware of the Cruisers Net, when, shortly after sunset, I lit up my charcoal grill on the deck of my steel battleship. From *Cockpit's* perspective it must have looked like *Seefalke* was hit by a torpedo amidst the peacefully anchored fleet. Pearl Harbor 2.0. For Mark to grab his fire extinguisher and jump into his dinghy was one. When he arrived and saw me peacefully having a barbecue rather than manning my anti-air guns, we had a good laugh. This is how I was introduced to the Isla Mujeres Cruisers Net.

With all the diversity we all have one thing in common. We all have time to clean, paint and empty our bilges (eh, reverse order I suppose works better) and it truly is amazing what comes to the surface. So the "Treasures of the Bilge" item becomes one of the funniest parts of the conference. It is so funny what people find, even funnier what they are looking for...

There are worse places to be stuck

Which is the perfect transition to the "Open Forum", the room for about anything, birthdays, anniversaries, jokes, anything, a place where we can forget about Corona for a few moments and stop watching our plans, by now C, D and E, getting flushed down the toilet.

"Channel 13 is now open as a hailing channel," Lisa wraps up today's conference. Maybe tomorrow I will jump in and make a distress announcement, asking to change to another but this calamitous channel number. It almost hurts my fingers to tune in to channel 13. I wonder why it is even on the radio. I pray to Neptune each day that Isla Mujeres Cruisers Net will not be broadcasting from Davy Jones' Locker one day.

It is the only thing that makes me a little worried these days. But just a little.

Lockdown Lunatics

This global lockdown had an impact. It had an impact not only on the world's economy and Mother Nature, it also had an impact on us people. Whereas some enjoyed the slowing down others feared for their existence. I was torn. On the one hand I feared for the existence of my business, on the other I enjoyed the clearing out of life's ballast. I had the feeling that finally, while the world was rumbling and tumbling I was able to see the essence of life.

In this mood I experienced the impressive astronomical event of the super moon. Please forgive me if I overdid it a bit.

Rise and Fall of Super Moon

I got up early this morning. I had my "good" camera charged overnight and I had researched that the moonset at my position here on Isla Mujeres, Mexico would be at 0707hrs UTC-5 or CDT (local time). Not too bad. But sunrise would already be at 0633hrs, so I knew I had to get up a good bit before that if I wanted to land a good shot.

It's a full moon, so for us earthlings the moon is opposite the sun but, as we just learned, not exactly. The sun rises a hair earlier than the moon sets. But more importantly, today the moon is close to its perigee and is supposed to appear almost 9% larger than usual. You better duck your head so close it will whoosh over it. The world calls this a supermoon. I call it showtime. I am sitting on the stern deck of my steel ketch *Seefalke*. It is elevated a bit and my favorite spot for astronomical observations. First row in my VIP box for the thrilling drama I am about to witness:

Cheerfully playing in the skies

Last night I watched the sun cheerfully playing in the skies, as if there was no tomorrow. Carefree and wild, like a paint spilling child, she plunged the world into always changing colors, for no specific reason, just because she could.

Dangerously close to the edge

While the sun was playing lightheadedly, coming dangerously close to the edge of the horizon the moon was sneaking into the playground. Silently, inwardly, covertly, still pale and in full camouflage while the world was distracted by the loud light-show in the West. Generously, he would grant the sun her final show, like a delinquent is granted a last cigarette. This night would be his night. He knew it. He was supermoon. The world's eyes would be on him. It would just take a little bit of patience until the sun would burn in her own vanity.

The fireball is tumbling and falling of the edge into eternity

And while the glowing fireball is tumbling, eventually falling off the edge into eternity, the moon rises higher and higher, humbly, yet aware of his silent might. He needs no colors to emphasize his power. Understatement is his credo. Black and white is just enough. He controls our dreams. Oceans follow his course in obedient loyalty. Million stars step back in awe-stricken reverence when he arrives at the scene. The skies are all his.

Unparalleled. Undefeated. Undisputed. The supermoon reaches his zenith. The firmament is his palace. The world is his oyster. But now, early in the morning, it is him for whom the bell tolls, and he knows it. With my telephoto right on his face I feel like a paparazzi, like a voyeur, denying him the last bit of privacy in the blackest hour of this proud sovereign.

As he descends, calmly stepping down towards the cliff that soon he is condemned to jump off from, he grows one last time. He raises his head and proudly watches towards the East, calmly expecting his joyful hangman. He is ready.

No fear. No worries. No resentment.

Gracefully he uses his power one last time to move the clouds and block the view at the moment of death.

At 0707hrs it is done.

I take down my camera, slowly, moved by the moment. The sunrise is beautiful but I don't feel like taking photos anymore.

"Hey, that was just a beautiful moonset," I try to cheer myself up a little. I smile to myself.

“Yes, maybe it was. But maybe it was the rise and fall of supermoon. Maybe it was a metaphor for our very existence.”

Then I take my clothes off and jump into the sea. I feel the warm water surrounding my body and my soul. I feel alive. Life is beautiful.

All photos were taken at Isla Mujeres between the evening of April 8th and the morning of April 9th, 2020.

Farewell to Prohibition

Normally in the Bahia of Isla Mujeres there is a continual coming and going of boats. It is a popular stop on the way south to the hurricane safe locations of Guatemala and Panama or north to the US and Canada. This year, however, Isla Mujeres is static. Weeks pass without a boat arriving or departing. The borders around Mexico are closed and no one wants to take the risk to become a ghost ship drifting about in the seven seas without being able to call in a port.

So it was an extraordinary event when the crew of *S/V Shaula*, a proud Italian ketch, finally decided to set sail. They knew that officially no port on the way was open and they planned for a nonstop passage at a time when Italy was in total lockdown. There was more than one head being shaken in sheer disbelief at the bravery (or stupidity) of those Italians. Maybe it was just their wine running low that forced them to leave.

It was prohibition after all...

A Tale of Tears and Treasure

Part 1: The Tears

The lighthouse, a distinct landmark approaching Isla Mujeres

I shake Tommaso's, Michele's and Renato's hands. Screw social distancing for a moment!

"Fair winds! Stay safe! See you later in this life or the next!"

A smile. A hug. A nod. I see tears glitter in their eyes. I climb down the rope ladder into my bright red dinghy. I crank my little Mercury outboard and set off to head back to my anchorage. We have known each other since Havana. *S/V Shaula* was docked right next to *S/V Seefalke* in Marina Hemingway. At a time when the marinas in Cuba were still open. At a time when the stores still had food. At a time when the only source of headache was the hangover after another night full of rum, cigars and salsa.

S/V Shaula and S/V Seefalke in Havana

Just 300 nautical miles and a few months away, in pre-Corona post-revolutionary Cuba it feels like this was in a different life. It sure was a different world. But as the world turns and burns and rumbles and tumbles, we sailors remain the same. We keep moving in the continuous rhythm of the winds and the currents, like driving on seasonal roads. No sailor is stupid enough to go offroad. A lesson each sailor learns at the very beginning of his career. Mostly these are painful lessons, hence effective and lasting. So we are bound to meet again, sooner or later.

But then there also are these crossroads where Mother Nature allows a turn. *Shaula* decided to pick her up on the offer now. We sailors have a very special attitude towards parting. The essence of our existence is to see new places, meet new people, and make new experiences. The nature of our mode of travel dictates that we can only see the new if we leave the old behind. This is a great difference to land people. For them parting is mostly something forced, something involuntary and sad, whereas for us sailors it is a deliberate and free decision. Very rarely do you see sailors with tears in their eyes when they part. It is because parting is when we start to look forward to seeing each other again. This time *Shaula's* crew has tears in their eyes though, but they are not for me.

The wind is fierce today, six Beaufort, gusting seven. As I am trying to make way against the wind, the waves are crashing against my little dinghy and the spray is brutally hitting my face. I feel like someone is lashing me with the cat-o-nine tails, again and again. After two minutes I am soaked to the bone, my eyes are red and swollen from salt water and my dinghy is turned into a barely floating rubber bathtub performing a crazy rodeo. The marine version. I feel like I am riding a mad killer whale, stung by a Portuguese man-of-war. While I am trying to bail out the water from the dinghy and at the same time trying to keep my face from getting slapped and smacked all over again, I have a hard time manoeuvring this little sucker through the breaking waves. I think of what lies ahead of the three Italians of *Shaula*.

They decided to sail from Mexico to Italy, hoping on a stop in the Azores but planning for a nonstop passage. Hope for the best, be prepared for the worst. Their route will take them out of the Caribbean Sea through the Yucatan Channel into the Mexican Gulf, then through the Straits of Florida, past Bermuda into the open Atlantic. Then past the Azores through the Straits of Gibraltar into the Mediterranean Sea and somewhere to Italy. Where exactly they don't know yet. This will depend on the situation when they get there. Will Italy still be in lockdown after the 40 to 50 day passage? No one can tell. A passage with an unknown destination and an uncertain destiny. Nothing for the faint hearted.

S/V Shaula at Isla Mujeres

But *Shaula's* crew is everything but faint hearted. They have carefully analyzed the very complex situation. They evaluated their options between Corona lockdowns and hurricanes, ocean crossings and safe havens and calmly took their decision: We are sailing home. They took on fuel, water, and provisions. They are ready. If it wasn't for that one little detail. A detail that is capable of wetting those tough sailors‘ eyes.

Whereas alcohol is still sold in many places on the mainland, here on Isla Mujeres we actually live under prohibition. Alcohol sales at supermarkets and stores has been suspended for many weeks now and bars were closed long ago. The walkways to the bars and restaurants are covered in dust and sand. It looks a little like it had snowed all night. The booze tanks on the boats at the anchorage are drier than Death Valley in the summer and not a few sailors seem to be going cold turkey. Alcoholics anonymous at sea so to speak. Others, so the rumors, have used their time, creativity, and unused spare parts to turn their boats into floating distilleries or breweries. The mother of invention is having babies. The less technically oriented sailors have used their underground channels to traffic the liquid gold to the island. They are easily identifiable by an increased cockroach population. Tell me how many cockroaches you have and I tell you how much booze you smuggled.

Shaula went down the second route and got hold of three cases of best Dos Equis XX Lager Special bottled beer. 72 bottles of this golden liquid that at the moment out-values its solid equivalent by far as most breweries in Mexico suspended their production a few weeks ago. “So, where is the problem now?,“ you might ask. They have 72 bottles of beer for three people for a 40 day passage. This is one for each crew every other day, not too bad and they should be sober sailing anyway. All correct but here comes the caveat: the three cases of best Dos Equis Lager Special never made it to *Shaula* due to a series of unfortunate events.

On the way from the dock their heavily overloaded dinghy *T/T Shaula* broke apart in the wild surf, the inflatable hull came off the aluminum bottom and in a moment of weakness the crew chose the wrong priority. They first tried to rescue their own lives, then the outboard and by the time they were thinking about the beer it was already on its way to the Happy Brewery Grounds at the bottom of the Caribbean Sea. But who wants to blame them? Who wants to cast the first stone in this moment of hardship?

When I got their distress message on WhatsApp – it is obvious why they didn't want to use VHF – the magnitude of the disaster became clear to me momentarily. The *T/T Shaula* incident would easily make it to the top ten disasters in civil seafaring. So I cranked up my toy outboard and death defyingly rushed to the rescue. In the meantime they had moved their mother ship to the scene of the catastrophe less than a cable away from the Port Captain's dock, pretending they caught a rope in their prop. The depth is just five meters here, so there actually was a chance to retrieve the precious liquid.

Eventually the port captain got impatient and the Search-And-Rescue mission had to be aborted. After one hour of synchronous group snorkeling in front of his dock I don't think he bought the rope-in-the-prop explanation anymore. So, while *Shaula's* men are fighting their tears and I am fighting the same waves that broke *T/T Shaula's* back, the impressive ketch sets sail and the proud Italian flag slowly fades in the distance. I stay behind on treasure island with the burden of their legacy.

The treasure hunt is on.

A Tale of Tears and Treasure
Part 2: The Treasure

If you had to hide something really well, where would that be? Something valuable or dangerous maybe, or compromising, when you would need to make sure the wrong people will never find it. Your obsolete bio-weapon, COVID lab equipment maybe, or the unfortunate remains of your lover's husband, or your recent unauthorized bank withdrawal. Yes, exactly. You want it to vanish from the face of the earth. But when you do your homework you will find that underground is too risky. You hardly can do it without leaving evidence on the surface. They have drones nowadays that can detect if earth was moved, and make no mistake, trained dogs can smell up to five meters underground. Also, on land things can change quickly. When you get out of jail eventually your treasure might be underneath a skyscraper or someone whose karma was better than yours donated the results of your hard work to the local gardeners association. I would easily bet the best part of the aforementioned bank withdrawal that sooner or later you will consider underwater options, especially if you plan to come back and retrieve it one day. Underwater is so much better. No trails, no dogs, no drones. No construction projects, no lucky gardeners. Just water and sharks. Those sharks will thankfully help you with your lover's husband

and they will guard your fresh cash, too. I don't know how they feel about decommissioned COVID labs though. Anyway, underwater is a good alternative. There must be a reason that many intercontinental ballistic missiles with nuclear warheads are installed on submarines. If it wasn't for this one little caveat: What goes for others also goes for you. Underwater treasures are hard to find and even harder to retrieve. Especially if you don't exactly remember where you put them. Especially when currents and tides are helping with the hide rather than the seek.

Now I am sitting in the navigation corner of my boat *S/V Seefalke* racking my brains. The depth in the target area is just 15 to 18 ft but the wind is still churning up the water, making a treasure hunt impossible. Relief is in the forecast but only in two days. So I have two more days to make a plan. The countdown is on. The countdown is on for two reasons. First, I am concerned that the current that mainly sets in one direction only will slowly bury the treasure forever underneath a pile of sand. And second, my Italian friends, well, I thought they were my friends, left a message on our local cruisers' net Facebook group that raised people's attention. It said: "Maik knows a little secret that might be of some delight for a lucky diver." So I have to expect competition. Thank you very much, Michele! Also I need to take the Port Captain into consideration. I cannot afford to raise his suspicion again. The good news however, is that in two days it will be Sunday, and the Port Captain's office is closed on Sundays. So, if I want to be successful, and my own ambition will not allow any other outcome, I have to be fast and effective. My fantasies take wing and fly. Really high. I get dressed, my face is painted green. Then I swiftly crawl out of the torpedo tube of the submarine that brought me here at night. I use the newest underwater scooter that takes me to ground zero. Within a few minutes I have found and retrieved the treasure and returned back to my submarine mothership. My name will never be mentioned but the honor will be mine and mine only. Still in my inebriety of the excitement of anticipation I try to recall the mottos of the world's best special forces. I think I will need to combine them all. I need to be "fast and heavy" as the Russian Speznaz, "strong and guileful" like the British SAS and with the "decisive will" of the German KSK. So, eventually "it will pay to be a winner" like the US Navy SEALS. Of course in my defense I want to emphasize that their budgets are slightly higher than mine and their tasks are usually much easier.

Back on sea level I have to admit to myself that I would probably not qualify for any of those elite units and that I may be a good swimmer but certainly not a great diver. Also the search area is right between the ferry terminal and the navy base. In absence of a submarine scooter, chances are good I get knocked over by one of the high-speed ferries or the coast guard ship without them even noticing. I need a wingman. I don't like this idea but it is the bitter truth. So I share my secret with Günther from *S/V Acapulco* and also Andreas from *S/V Chibidarra* and Steffen from *S/V Argo* are standing by. Sunday will be D-Day. No wind, no current, no Port Captain. Perfect. On Sunday in the early morning the radio comes alive. It is Günther with a coded message:

„Captain Flint, Captain Flint this is Long John Silver. The water is clear. Over."

„This is Captain Flint. Roger. Out."

The rest of the anchorage is still asleep when I load my dinghy with my GPS tracker, a marking buoy, a retrieval anchor, some lines and my snorkel equipment and head over to *S/V Acapulco*, a beautiful 57 foot sloop from Hamburg, Germany. I wish I had a silent running stealth mode. It feels like I would wake up the entire anchorage with the deafening noise of my outboard motor. Long John Silver is already waiting for me. He has his scuba gear ready. Just in case. We quickly load everything into his dinghy that is much bigger than mine and transit to our designated operation area.

Gear is ready for the mission

When we arrive we notice a navy soldier on the pier, watching us with great tactical interest. If you can't defeat your enemy, make him your friend. So we decide to give him a heads-up. We tell him a slightly modified version of the truth and he is fine. Then we go back to ground zero and anchor the dinghy. Long John Silver takes the port side, Captain Flint starboard. Our search pattern is 90 ft in one direction then 18 ft on the opposite course back again and again and again. Loop after loop. After a little less than two hours we have covered an area of approximately 30,000 square feet, but we have found nothing. Nada. Niente. No, I don't want to lie to you, we found a few tires, a fridge, a pipe and something that looked like a part of an airplane wing. But no beer.

But our skin is cured and pickled and I am sure we have completely satisfied our Natrium demands for the rest of our lives when we crawl back into the dinghy and retreat from the search area, exhausted and a bit frustrated, too. Fast and heavy? Not really. Strong and guileful? Not anymore. A decisive will? Maybe this is what is left at least. We are Germans after all.

The navy pier: wrong search area

A little later I see a few dinghies searching closer to the navy pier. Way too far upstream I think and relax. I sit in my navigation corner again and I continue to re-evaluate the search area. We searched where the Italians thought they lost their beer. Most probably they remembered it where they thought they were at the time of the accident. But probably they have not taken into consideration sinking rate and current. And also they drifted some time on their wrecked dinghy before the beer went overboard.

But the Italians are not to be trusted. Maybe they put up a huge show. Maybe they are now laughing their asses off and having OUR beer in the middle of the Atlantic! But let‘s stick with Sherlock Holmes: “Once you eliminate the impossible, whatever remains, no matter how improbable, must be the truth.“

We are talking about glass bottles full of a liquid with the same density as water. With a little air, too, because the bottles are not filled to the rim. The glass, again, is slightly more dense than water. It sank, this means the buoyancy was not enough to make it float. However, the sinking rate must have been extremely low. But the current at the time of the incident was strong. So it must have drifted a considerable distance downstream before it hit rock bottom. And there it strikes me. Suddenly I understand where we have to search. It strikes me right in the face. It is the most dangerous and most uncomfortable place. Nobody had searched there yet, not the Italians, not us, no one else who was out there. Because there cannot be what is not supposed to be, and Sherlock Holmes is right again.

So, in the late afternoon we give it another try. This time with *S/V Chibidarra*, my Swedish friends. They are high-tech equipped with echo sounder and GPS. This time we don‘t anchor the dinghy but Andreas is dragging Anders and Hanna behind the dinghy (Please don‘t do this at home!), while I am the wild card and search the area that struck my mind: right in front of the ferry port entry. Once I really think this is it, as one of the catamaran high-speed ferries backs out of the harbor heading right for me. But luckily it turns and heads the other way before its propellers make mincemeat out of me. We sure are braver than we are smart. It takes a while until I can breath again and my heart rate is back in the two-digit area. But who wants to live forever anyway and not everyone has the pleasure of dying doing something that makes the world a better place.

Ground zero

And hey, is there something? Yes, I think there is something. It does not look like a beer case but it certainly looks like one of those heavy duty IKEA bags full of bottles. I flag down my Swedish friends and Anders is the first to dive to the bottom and lift up the bag. It is far lighter than what we all expected, yes, my buoyancy calculation was right. The bottles were just marginally heavier than water. Only when we lifted it up to Andreas in the dinghy suddenly the bag turned heavy and we all had to help pushing it up. The curse of the Italians? Or just physics? Then Hanna, who swam a few meters ahead, calls us.

“Here is more!“

We swim to her and Anders is the first at the bottom again. This time however, the bag seems to be much heavier. Anders is visibly struggling to lift it. Then I see the bag is anchored to the ground, at least it looks like that. So I go down and retrieve a small dinghy anchor and a trolley. The bag, the trolley, and the dinghy anchor are all tangled in the anchor line but together we manage to securely save the second part of the treasure. The third bag is kindergarten.

We are exhausted, almost too weak to pull ourselves back into the dinghy. But we are euphoric. We simply can‘t stop laughing and not believing it. We found the fucking needle in the haystack. No, better! We found 72 bottles of Dos Equis XX Lager Special on the bottom of the sea. It took them 73 years to find one Titanic, it took us less than one day to find 72 bottles of beer!

Victory!

Then we take the mandatory victory selfie and head back to the anchorage to begin our victory parade. We decide to share the treasure with everyone who helped (or competed with) us. We go from boat to boat and drink and laugh and celebrate until the last bottle is filled with air and its buoyancy is changed for good. Just making sure this does not happen again.

Tomasso, Michele, Renato, I know you are still on the high seas of the Atlantic Ocean. Thank you for making our day. I swear every single bottle was dedicated to you guys and never have so many people thought of you and wished you a save voyage. With all your sacrifice I am convinced the winds will never be fairer and the seas will never be more following than on this passage.

Before this I had never drank beer in my entire life. So all it took was prohibition and a treasure hunt.

The Other Mexico

Let me tell you this: I love Mexico and my Mexican friends. I do not believe that Mexico is a country of corrupt politicians, brutal gangs and powerful drug cartels. Well, not only. There is also that other Mexico. The Mexico of impressive cultural heritage, immense natural diversity, the Mexico of unbelievable kind and compassionate people, the Mexico that kept its doors open while all others' were closed. But when you are in Mexico long enough, sooner or later you will also catch a glimpse into the dark side of this compelling place.

The following story consists of two parts, "Humiliation" and "Retaliation". Whereas in part one you have to live with what I left you, in part two you can again ***choose your fate*** and make your own decisions. Again, if you prefer to read the original, based on facts, then jump to "Mexican Standoff - Part 2: Retaliation - Original", after you read part one.

Mexican Standoff
Part 1: Humiliation

I am wet. I am cold. My bruises hurt. My scrapes burn. My head aches. Breaded in sand like a schnitzel I feel hunger coming up. I take a deep drag. The sweet smoke befogs my mind and my sight but I still make out *Seefalke's* anchor light in the distance. So she is still there, her anchor holds.

Seefalke's lights in the distance

Already a little more relaxed, I pass the joint on to Ricardo, or was it Raul or Eduardo? Doesn't matter. All of a sudden he jumps up, as if stung by an adder, pointing the glowing stick into the dark and sputters:

"Hey, someone is signaling us from your boat!"

Worried about our smokable dinner, the only thing we have, I carefully take it off his trembling fingers, still stretched out, pointing to the ocean, before I explain:

"No, amigo, it's just the boat moving in the swell, I am all by myself."

"Ahh, ok." And after a short break: "But how will you get back to your boat then?", his voice is truly compassionate.

"Yes, this is the million dollar question.", I take another drag and *Seefalke's* light seems a bit less clear now, as if somebody just dimmed it a little.

Clearer, however, is the course of events that brought me into this unfortunate situation. Two days ago my friend Oliver whom I haven't seen forever (which technically is true because we only knew each other from Facebook) texted me and let me know that he and his family, on their odyssey back to their boat in Italy, had a one day layover in Cancún which is just a three hours sail from Isla Mujeres, my COVID quarantine home. They would stay at Crowne Paradiso hotel right at the beach in the south of Cancún's hotel zone.

A quick look at the chart shows me that this is a textbook no-go anchorage: a lee shore, totally open to the sea, exposed to wind and swell with a steep ocean bed that will certainly create an impressive surf. Yes, surfers would love it, I am sure. Sailors? Not so much. But the closest reasonable anchorage is miles away so I start negotiating with myself. Lazy tourist vs. experienced captain. It is a short fight the captain is doomed to lose. The arguments are compelling though: There have only been light winds for the last couple of days so no major swell is expected, accordingly the surf would be moderate and most likely manageable. Videos from the beach sent to me by my friend support these assumptions. Also it would only be for a couple of hours anyway. No harm, no foul. Easy peasy.

Never had I been so wrong.

Raul or Ricardo or Eduardo (I will just call him Ricardo from now on, I honestly don't remember his name, if he ever reads this he will forgive me) in slow motion falls back on his camping chair. I offer him our smoke but he just shakes his head. So I pass the joint to the other guy whose name I don't even try to remember. And so for a while my brand new beach buddies and me just sit there and stare into the night. Three complete strangers passing a joint and sharing saliva while the world is locked down behind face masks. It sure is something surreal. I feel a little nauseous – I am just not used to all that weed – and I feel the need to stretch my legs. So I get up and walk a few steps on the beach. The fresh night breeze feels good. I look up, a perfectly clear sky, beautiful. The Milky Way, Saturn and Jupiter, and a gazillion stars like in a planetarium, just real. Then still in awe and with my eyes up in the skies, I trip, I stumble, I fall. And while I am wondering who the hell put this huge rock in the middle of this meticulously clean beach, the rock moves its head and looks at me with big eyes and a friendly face. Was I that stoned already? From just a few drags of medium quality weed? Ok, yes, I am not used to it, I admit. But still… It takes a while, though, until I realize it is not a rock but a huge turtle. And while we look each other in the eyes, I am sober instantaneously. Then the turtle gives me one last smile before it turns its head and continues its cumbersome mission.

Cumbersome crawling on land

So graceful in their element

In a sailor's life the lows and highs really are close together. I slowly get up and then I realize that the entire beach is full of turtles. Amazing!! I can't identify them but they're approximately my size. Smaller than a Leatherback but much bigger than a Loggerhead, and still more and more are beaching, a D-Day like invasion. I love them. There is hardly any other animal that appears so peaceful and elegant. I once swam with Loggerhead turtles in Cabo Verde in West Africa. They don't swim, they fly, underwater though, gracefully gliding, swinging their fins like wings. They are not afraid but curious about this funny creature, awkwardly kicking its arms and legs to stay afloat: me. I remember I was so in awe that I totally forgot about the current and I had a hard time getting back to the beach.

On my way here I crashed a passionate turtle date as I was sailing. That was less elegant but quite funny. Hmmm, at least for me. I am sure they didn't appreciate it too much. I hope for them that they were still in the mood to continue what they started. Then I see one beaching. My eyes got used to the darkness and the moon just got over the horizon. A few powerful pulls gets the turtle on top of the wave and it surfs the wave like a boss and then gently touches down on the beach. Ten out of ten! But as soon as the turtle leaves her element all grace and elegance is gone and it is the turtle that turns into a funny creature, awkwardly kicking its fins to gain higher grounds. I remember my recent beaching experience that certainly was less graceful. One out of ten tops.

I arrive at my anchorage and against all odds the swell is significant. The tourist in me is surprised, the captain is pissed. He should have known better. It takes me two attempts until I find a spot that somewhat suits me. 1,200 ft from the beach the movements are bearable. I prepare myself and my dinghy for the ride, switch the anchor light on because I know I won't be back before sunset and crank the outboarder. I bought the dinghy just two days ago: an ancient self-made fiber-glass boat with a keel made from motorcycle parts. Very light, very stable in the water. It takes the waves well. As I approach the beach I feel the swell building up. The swell hits the rising seabed, the waves get higher and steeper. They break. Not good! And sooner than I expected I surf down the first wave, then the second. The third lifts me up and starts breaking. With breathtaking speed the beach comes closer and closer. It is a steep beach, must be low tide. I throttle my outboard, the wave makes a hissing noise as if it was laughing at me for my desperate attempt to slow down. I feel that if I would go just a little faster, I would take off and fly. And I feel the mental kick that surfers get rushing down the waves in insane speed. Stoked, is what they call it. Just I am not standing on a surfboard but sitting in a dinghy that would hardly survive the impact. And I am not too sure if I would survive the impact either. But at this time I kind of run out of choices. The impact is brutal. It is like the sea spits me out in a wild cough. As the dinghy hits the beach and comes to a sudden stop I am catapulted over the rim and onto the beach. Ouch that hurt. I get up as soon as my bruised body allows and start pulling the dinghy out of the surf, the next wave fills it with at least a quarter ton of water and it becomes an impossible task for me. But then I get some help. Four guys finally get the chance to use their beach bodies for something different than just posing for easily impressed bikini girls. They help me to pull the dinghy up the beach and with joint efforts we get it done. Not much in common with the graceful landing of my turtles.

I walk back to my brand new best friends, where I use the last two percent of my phone battery to send a message to Steve from *S/V Pili Aloha* that I won't make it to the morning cruisers' net radio conference that I was supposed to run the next morning. I send a second message to Günter from *S/V Acapulco* in case Pili Aloha would not look at their emails. Then I take a photo of my turtle friend and my phone dies. Ok, that was that. Then I fall on a beach lounge and get ready to sleep. I am still wet and covered in sand, a bit cold, too.

Ricardo brings me a blanket, dirty but warm. I accept it gratefully. No blanket could be dirty enough to make me any dirtier at this point.

Then I see one of the turtles getting back into the water. It looks so easy for them. What did I do wrong that those ancient creatures do so much better? I guess I am missing a few million years of evolution. After I secure the dinghy I walk up the beach and to the road that leads me to the hotel. Then the next unpleasant surprise: they don't let me in. And that is not because I am soaking wet or covered in sand or because maybe I look like a bum altogether. It is because of COVID, only hotel guests are allowed. (I do have the impression that the COVID excuse is very welcome though.) But they are sweet and recommend a restaurant nearby and a beach bar. My friend and I agree we would meet there and I head that way.

The only flaw in the plan is that both the restaurant and the beach bar are closed. So we end up just sitting at the beach chatting about this and that. A nice night, a fresh breeze, clear skies. But the swell is building up, not getting any better rising tide. Roll tide, roll, I remember Alabama's college football team's battle cry. I am starting to get worried. We count the waves. There is a rhythm: one big one, one a bit smaller, then four to five small ones. So the plan is to crank the motor, get the dinghy ready and after the somewhat smaller than the big one Olli would push the boat over it, I would hit gas and off I'd go. Once over the first surf I would be safe.

That is our plan.

So we get the dinghy ready and in position. However, the sea forgets about the rhythm for a moment obviously and after the big one there is another big one and another one and another one. The first one throws me out of the dinghy, the second one smashes the motor support into pieces. I barely manage to rescue the motor to the beach. Then I run back into the water to push the boat while Olli is pulling. It is almost completely filled with water by now. Then the undertow drags me into the sea until the next wave grabs me brutally and relentlessly and rolls me over and over again until the hurtful collision of my head with the dinghy forces me into an abrupt stop. I see stars, I swallow water, lots of it, I feel close to pass out and faint. A knockout. Well aimed.

My dinghy is ready and in position

"One, two, three...," I hear the referee counting me out.

Now that was a short fight. Knocked down in the first round. Even in my most pessimistic thoughts that was not what I had expected.

"Four, five...!" Not a good time!

"Six, seven...!" Not good at all!!

"Eight...!" What would Rocky do?

"Get up!!" I hear my crowd desperately cheering for me.

"Nine...!" As I feel the undertow grabbing me again, I finally get back on my feet and stumble up the beach.

Screw the dinghy, not worth it!! And no, swimming is not an option. Sometimes sailing is like boxing: It is not about how hard you can hit, it's about how hard you can get hit and keep moving forward. Olli and I sit down, soaking wet from sweat and seawater and we watch while the powerful seas crash my poor dinghy into pieces. Now I feel my bruises and scrapes burning in the salty water. Yes, the turtles sure do better!

I fall asleep. When I wake up the tropical sun is already burning down on me again. No turtles. Only their distinct trails in the sand prove it was not a dream. Then I see them. The jet skies. My ride!! My beach sleepover buddies tell me the jetski guys will be here sometime between 0900hrs and 1000hrs. So I wait patiently until the kids show up. We chat a little and I learn that they usually charge 55 USD for half an hour. But we need to wait for the boss because he is the man with the keys.

Then this fat guy enters the scene, and I know without telling that this is the boss. The kids brief him shortly and he turns to me:

"500 USD!"

First I think my Spanish turned from bad to worse overnight and I ask him if he meant 500 Pesos (approximately 25 USD) which sounded like a fair price to me. No, he meant 500 USD and this is what I would have to pay to get back to my boat. I thought a while until I felt it was appropriate to call him some names, a mix of Spanish and English but I think he got the point because all of a sudden the price drops to 100 USD. I offer him 50 USD instead:

"My last word."

"100 USD, my last word."

"Ok, here is the deal, 1,500 Pesos and you take me, my jerrycans and my motor."

After a short hesitation he agrees and we load the jerry cans on one of the jet skies. The motor does not fit but they will come back with it. Once back on my boat I realize that they have little reason to come back with my motor. And they must have had the exact same thought because nobody is coming back with my motor. Something tells me they had this thought long before me. After some 20 minutes of helpless waiting I weigh anchor and set sail. It must look graceful from the beach. They have to give me that! Sometimes you win, sometimes you lose. I admit defeat. For now.

But I will be back!

The following story is a ***Choose your Fate Story*** again. If you prefer to read the original version without multiple choices continue reading on page 247.

Choose Your Fate:

Mexican Standoff

Part 2: Retaliation - 0

So I lost my dinghy, I got bruised and hurt, I spent the night in the dirt, I got ripped-off and robbed. Humiliated. How deep can you fall and still not hit rock bottom? Once again I remember Rocky's words:

"It's not about how hard you hit, it's about how hard you can get hit and keep moving forward!"

And yes, I keep moving forward. A light breeze blows from the East. It will be a broad reach back to Isla Mujeres. Four to five hours, I guess. Slowly, like a freight train, my heavy steel ketch sets off. It takes a while until we finally reach our admittedly low cruising speed. But I am not in a hurry. About halfway to Punta Cancún I get hailed on VHF channel 16, the international emergency and hailing channel:

"Seefalke, Seefalke for Acapulco, over."

Was that really *Acapulco*? My neighbors at my anchorage at Isla Mujeres? My quarantine buddies? My friends Conny and Günter coming to my rescue?

S/V Acapulco coming for my rescue

"Acapulco, this is *Seefalke*, over," comes my formal reply.

We Germans are known for keeping a minimum of radio discipline even when everyone else doesn't. However, we are not as bad as the British.

"Channel 69?"

"69"

On channel 69 I learn that it was only in the morning that they read the message I sent to them last night, with my last remaining phone battery. Then they immediately set sail to come to my rescue. They figured my phone was dead and I wouldn't be able to reply. We agree to meet behind the reef of Punta Cancún, anchor there and catch up. It takes another two hours until I get there as the wind almost dies on me completely. But then my anchor, after Tropical Storm Cristobal its name is Cristo, is dropped just three boat lengths from *Acapulco.*

Rendezvous with S/V Acapulco

I jump into the warm and crystal clear water and swim over to them. We have a coffee and I tell my story, how I wanted to see my friend, how the surf destroyed my dinghy, the turtles, the jet skies, the betrayal, the humiliation. As I finish Conny is the first to speak:

"Don't let them have your motor! You need to get it back! It's not only about the motor, it's a question of honor! Don't let them get away with it!"

And Günter adds:

"But you have to do it now. Otherwise the motor will be gone for good. Time is a critical factor. Every hour counts."

I am not too convinced, looking at the facts that I am outnumbered badly, they are well connected with the local police, and I am not too keen to get beaten up by a Mexican beach gang.

But Günter insists:

"We will have lunch now. But if you have the balls I'll take you to the beach, then get a taxi and get your motor back! You will think of something, I'm sure!"

Of course I have balls, I just have my doubts that they will be of much use during this operation. At the end of the day it is just a motor!

What should I do?

If you decide to give up and leave them your motor continue reading on page 231 (section 1.1)

If you decide to fight and try to get your motor back continue reading on page 233 (section 1.2)

Choose Your Fate:

Mexican Standoff

Part 2: Retaliation - 1.1

You decided to quit because your life is worth more than a motor.

But Günter insists:

“We will have lunch now. But if you have the balls I’ll take you to the beach, then get a taxi and get your motor back! You will think of something, I’m sure!” Of course I have balls, I just have my doubts that they will be of much use during this operation. At the end of the day it is just a motor!

What should I do?

They talk the talk but would they walk the walk? No! They talk the talk but the one who ultimately needs to walk the walk is me and me alone. It is just a little motor, 2.5 hp. I remember I bought it in Vigo, Spain because my first mate had difficulties handling the oars at the time. It was a good decision and it was a good deal, too. I think I paid 800 EUR for it.

So should I really risk my life for 800 EUR? On the other hand, hey, should I leave them *my* motor? Should audacity really win here? Would I be able to look at myself in the mirror if I let them get away with it?

But am I here to evangelize Mexico? Should I try what generations of police, military, and politicians could not accomplish - or die trying?

Nope! I have other plans. Sometimes smartness comes dressed as a coward. I know I am not a coward, just taking the only reasonable decision. So I just look at Conny and Günter and slowly shake my head:

"I don't think I should risk a war with a Mexican beach gang over an 800 EUR outboard motor. Let's enjoy life! Let's go snorkeling at this reef here. I heard it's beautiful."

First they look at me slightly puzzled but then Conny nods:

"That's probably smart. And yes, let's go snorkeling!"

And so we all jump in the water and set off to that reef. The current is hefty but eventually we make it and the underwater world is breathtaking!! So much better than fighting with a Mexican gang! There are giant turtles and fish in all colors of the rainbow, barracudas of our size but also I think I saw a shark in the distance. So we calmly head back to our boats, so much easier with the current pushing. Then we weigh anchor and sail home to Isla in the fresh evening breeze.

Life is good!

Choose Your Fate:
Mexican Standoff
Part 2: Retaliation - 1.2

You have decided to fight for your motor.

But Günter insists:

"We will have lunch now. But if you have the balls I'll take you to the beach, then get a taxi and get your motor back! You will think of something, I'm sure!"

Of course I have balls. I just have my doubts that they will be of much use during this operation. At the end of the day it is just a motor!

What should I do?

They talk the talk but would they walk the walk? No! They talk the talk but the one who ultimately needs to walk the walk is me and me alone. It is just a little motor, 2.5 hp. I remember I bought it in Vigo, Spain because my first mate had difficulties handling the oars at the time. It was a good decision and it was a good deal, too. I think I paid 800 EUR for it. So should I really risk my life for 800 EUR? On the other hand, hey, should I leave them *my* motor? Should audacity really win here? Would I be able to look at myself in the mirror if I let them get away with it?

NEVER!!

I would rather rest in an unmarked grave than surrender! After lunch Günter takes me to the closest beach and I get a taxi back to Playa Delfines, the scene of this morning's defeat, my personal Waterloo. I pay the taxi driver half of the agreed price and ask him to wait for me. It wouldn't take more than half an hour, one way or the other.

As I walk down the dunes I have a perfect view on the scene. Officially the beach is still closed so there are no civilians, just my enemy and me. Perfect for an honorable standoff, no collateral damages, only combatants. Just the numbers make me worry: I count eleven opponents. So I sure wouldn't win this by muscle power, also I am sure my fire power is to my disadvantage. I don't know theirs but I know mine is zero. But I have the element of surprise to my advantage and I figure they don't want too much noise among the hotels. This is where they recruit their rip-off victims. Also I am mad and pumped with adrenaline which makes me unpredictable. So all in all I think the odds are about even. At first nobody pays attention as I descend the dunes towards the beach. But as I come closer they see and recognize me, staring at me like they've seen a ghost. Where there once was chatter, talking, and laughter, now all of a sudden there is silence and tension and all twenty-two eyes follow every single one of my movements.

I try to make out that fat man, the boss. And there I see him, sitting in a camping chair in the shade of a beach pavilion. In normal no-COVID times tourists would get their sun-screen-soaked bodies treated by swift hands here. It would smell of sunscreen and oil, soap and vacation. Now it is the boss's headquarters. It smells of sweat, garlic, and chilies. I enter the chief's tent through a curtain of hostility. I walk straight up to him. I am a friend of words, I am writing essays after all. But this time I keep it short and sweet. Ok, perhaps not too sweet and admittedly neither exceedingly friendly nor particularly diplomatic:

"Hey asshole, where is my motor?"

His surprised face couldn't be more real. A great actor! I wouldn't want to play poker with him. But the game has already started. Can't bail out anymore at this point.

"Which motor, amigo?," he asks with a conciliatory smile.

"I am not your amigo and I want my motor back now, you d... sucking mother f... son of a b...," I didn't even make the effort to show a poker face.

As my Spanish is not good enough yet for impressive swearing, I spice it up with some English. Not too sure if he understands the details of the sexual abnormalities they imply for him to be involved in but I am sure he gets the point.

"I don't know anything about your motor. But let me help you amigo."

"Has anyone seen my friend's motor?," he raises his voice so that the entire gang can hear it.

Everybody is shaking their heads in perfectly synced choreography, some with a smirk. I am desperately outnumbered. Calling the atmosphere hostile is a blunt understatement. They do not seem ready to give in and the motor is nowhere to be seen. I feel like I am losing the situation, running out of options.

I could bluff to burn down their beach club but that would be a high-risk strategy. Or, I could go to the police. I have seen a little police station on top of the dunes at the beach parking. But there is honor among thieves and I do not trust the police much more than my beach buddies down here. I remember someone mentioned last night that 'he could call his brother in law who works at the police' to help me. So, no doubt, they are well connected. But maybe that is still the better option than to go for an impudent bluff. On the other hand perhaps audacity needs to be answered with audacity.

But I have to act fast.

If you decide to go to the police continue reading on page 237 (section 1.2.1)

If you decide to bluff continue reading on page 241 (section 1.2.2)

Choose Your Fate:

Mexican Standoff

Part 2: Retaliation - 1.2.1

You decided to go to the police.

I am desperately outnumbered. Calling the atmosphere hostile is a blunt understatement. They do not seem ready to give in and the motor is nowhere to be seen. I feel like I am losing the situation, running out of options.

I could bluff to burn down their beach club but that would be a high-risk strategy. Or, I could go to the police. I have seen a little police station on top of the dunes at the beach parking. But there is honor among thieves and I do not trust the police much more than my beach buddies down here. I remember someone mentioned last night that 'he could call his brother in law who works at the police' to help me. So, no doubt, they are well connected. But maybe that is still the better option than to go for an impudent bluff. On the other hand perhaps audacity needs to be answered with audacity. But I have to act fast.

I think the police might be the safer bet. I hardly can imagine that they openly collaborate with these third-class gangsters here. So I make my strategic withdrawal and retreat to the dunes. Up on the parking lot I already see the police car. My Spanish is not quite fluent yet, but it is good enough to explain my problem. The officers listen to me with great interest and they are ready to join me and go back to the beach.

As we arrive they are greeted very respectfully. A touch too respectfully if you ask me. I have never seen Mexicans treat police this way, so a feeling comes up that this is all a great show and I am the only guest. I hear them asking about my motor but then I lose them. They start speaking so fast and in a dialect that I cannot follow at all. After some back and forth one of the officers turns to me and asks me, slowly and in a completely understandable Spanish:

"Can you prove that they stole your motor?"

I tell them the short version of my story again but need to admit that neither can I prove anything nor do I have witnesses other than them. The officer patiently listens and seems very compassionate. But then he shrugs his shoulders:

"Señor, if you cannot prove it and have no witnesses, I really cannot do anything. Maybe it was somebody else entirely. We can take your report up in our car but I can't give you much hope that we will find your motor."

Yes, I do believe that! And while I am thinking if I should make the effort of making a report, someone points at the wreck of my dinghy and says something I don't understand. The police officer turns back to me and says:

"You need to take your trash, too. What happened is unfortunate but you cannot leave this beach like that."

I try to explain to him that yesterday they seemed very happy about my dinghy and that they wanted to keep and fix it. But, of course, nobody can remember this. So, the police officer offers:

"You have two choices: you can take your dinghy and there will be no charges for trespassing, because this beach is officially closed. Or we need to organize its disposal which will cost you 3,000 Pesos."

He knows there is no way I can take this dinghy right now, and in my mind I already start kicking my ass for even going to the police. I could have been snorkeling and enjoying the afternoon with Conny and Günter, but now I need to pay 3,000 pesos for not getting my motor back. I give up. Reluctantly I hand him six 500 Pesos and without a further word I turn around, walk up the dunes, return to my taxi that is still waiting and call it a day.

Obviously I have not been in this country long enough to know all the rules yet.

Choose Your Fate:

Mexican Standoff

Part 2: Retaliation - 1.2.2

You decided to go for a bluff.

"Has anyone seen my friend's motor?," he raises his voice so that the entire gang can hear it.

Everybody is shaking their heads in perfectly synced choreography, some with a smirk. I am desperately outnumbered. Calling the atmosphere hostile is a blunt understatement. They do not seem ready to give in and the motor is nowhere to be seen. I feel like I am losing the situation, running out of options.

I could bluff to burn down their beach club but that would be a high-risk strategy. Or, I could go to the police. I have seen a little police station on top of the dunes at the beach parking. But there is honor among thieves and I do not trust the police much more than my beach buddies down here. I remember someone mentioned last night that 'he could call his brother in law who works at the police' to help me. So, no doubt, they are well connected. But maybe that is still the better option than to go for an impudent bluff. On the other hand perhaps audacity needs to be answered with audacity. But I have to act fast.

Yes, I am desperately outnumbered but I am mad and I am pumped. I walk up to where all his jet skies are lined up. I know that they leave them there overnight, just covered with a piece of canvas. I jump on the newest model, patting it tenderly, like a horse:

"Maybe it would help your memory if I burn down one of your jet skies?," I address the boss with my sweetest, most loving, tender voice.

"Maybe two, you never know. You took my motor but you left me my two jerrycans of gasoline. That would make a fantastic beach fire, don't you think? Let's meet again tomorrow, maybe you'll remember my motor, then?"

"Tranquilo, amigo!"

"No, no tranquilo and no amigo. Let's get this straight. We'll be friends again as soon as I get my motor back but until then, I am gonna torch your jet skies, one after another, night by night," I jump off the saddle.

Despite all the tension I must smile amused as I picture his face waking up with the charred handlebar of his favorite jet ski next to him in his bed. The Godfather would be proud of me! Also I am grateful he is renting out jet skies and not horses. He smiles his most innocent smile and says:

"Hey, I now do remember your motor but we brought it to your boat, didn't we?!"

"Well, that's progress but nope, you didn't. You brought me to my boat but not my motor. Don't try to bullshit a bullshitter!"

Then I make out the kid who was my driver this morning:

"Hey, do you remember me?"

"Yes."

"Do you remember bringing me to my boat?"

"Yes."

"Good. Now do you remember bringing my motor to my boat?"

"Hmm, you need to talk to my boss."

"I am talking to you. Do you remember bringing my motor to my boat?"

"Please! Talk to my boss!," he pleads splattering.

That is enough confession for me. I go back to the boss:

"Listen, we can do this the hard way. I torch your bar, your jet skies and I swear to all Maya gods, I will turn this beach into a battlefield as Cancún has not seen it before. I have friends who just love this stuff.," comes my convincing bluff.

"And honestly, I would enjoy this, too. (I actually really would!) Maybe I lose, but do you want to take that risk for a ridiculous 3 HP outboard motor? Do you really want a war? Or, we'll be all reasonable and friends again. And you will never hear from me again and you can keep ripping off gringos in peace until the end of time."

Then I decide to play the Germany card, I know that many Mexicans secretly admire Germany for the hard time we gave the Americans in WWII.

"We Germans have neither conscience nor remorse. You better not upset a German. We keep our words. We don't play. Go play with the gringos, they are easier prey anyway. Doesn't this sound appealing?"

He walks a few steps towards another closed beach bar. One of those that has swings instead of chairs. He sits on a swing and waves me to take the swing beside him. He is thinking. This is a good sign. I sit down and he offers me a beer. It is cold. I can see drops of condensate running down the can. Despite being German I don't like beer but for the sake of the negotiation I take it and open the can. So we sit a while, swinging, sipping our beers, watching out into the ocean, like year-long best buddies hanging out, having a good time.

The rest of the crowd remains in respectful distance, eyeballing us. The open hostility is gone but the tension is tangible. The boss is still thinking. I see what he wants. He wants a solution that doesn't make him lose his face, and he doesn't want a big fuss about all this. Then he obviously has an idea:

"Amigo, didn't you tell us to take care of your motor and to keep it for a while until you'd be back?"

Smart guy after all. So I play along:

"Absolutely. And now I am back and would like to pick it up. And if you did what we agreed you'd do, I'd certainly consider a tip," I bluntly offer a ransom.

He smiles. I smile. Finally we are talking the same language. Two battle-experienced street-smart bullshitting field marshals preventing WWIII with a trick. The leaders of the world could learn from us. No one needs to die. All it takes are two swings, two beers, and the will to find a solution. We keep drinking our beers, swinging relaxed. We even do some small talk. He shows me photos of his wife and his kids on his smartphone. Sweet family. Maybe this fat arrogant asshole is a nice guy in his civilian life. We agree on a 1,000 Pesos tip. Then he makes a phone call and two guys carry my motor and, as a bonus, my little manual drainage pump and carefully put them down on one of the beach lounges. We shake hands.

"Amigos?"

"Amigos!" We hug.

We bump our fists. The ultimate gesture of peace and understanding.

"You need to leave this beach now," an unfriendly voice barks at me from behind. I turn my head into the direction of that voice and ask the boss "Now who is this clown?"

"He is the park ranger," he replies visibly annoyed. That was not planned.

I have my doubts, though. The "park ranger's" uniform looks like he bought it in a carnival store and he clearly doesn't have the authority of an official. Also I saw him cleaning one of the jetskies earlier. My personal guess is that this guy plays the park ranger whenever one of the gringos they want to rip off makes trouble. And this time the boss was just too late to let him know the beach poker was over. He builds up in front of me and says:

"This beach is closed to the public and you have to leave now."

"I am finishing my beer and then I leave these holy grounds for good – with my motor. Relax!"

"You will need to prove to me that this is your motor!"

"If you clown can show me a valid ID I will prove to you that I am the emperor of the united kingdom of Mexico and Germany but until then, I am no longer talking to you at all."

The boss gives him a reluctant nod and he sets off and returns with a piece of paper in a plastic foil. He awkwardly presents it to me. In an unexpected rapid move I rip it out of his hands, look at it for a glance and then I lose it. I just can't help it. I start laughing and simply can't stop. Laughing so hard I fall off my swing and into the sand. Gasping for air I get back on my feet and sit down on my swing again. That was just the worst fake ID I have ever seen. The photo was a selfie shot, the ID No. was a row of zeros and the Mexican flag was printed the wrong way, like inverted. So, not green, white, red but red, white, green with the eagle and the snake upside down. I mean for Christ's sake, they could have put just a little more effort into this! When I finally have enough air to talk again I hand the boss 500 Pesos:

"You just lost half of your tip. I am sorry. No, I'm really not, but if you want to have my advice as an amigo: You better invest it in some better fake IDs!"

Then I stand up, take my motor and my pump and climb up those steep dunes to the parking lot. I hold the motor in my arms like a baby, damn heavy. I resist the urge to relocate that massive bastard. I won't give them that satisfaction. I also resist the urge to turn around. If they want to kill me now they have to shoot me in the back like cowards. But Mexicans are too proud to do that. Also I don't think any of them are such a good shot. However, I am a bit surprised as I make it to the parking lot with no bullets in my back. The taxi is still waiting for me.

The only worries I have now are if I would remember all the details for my story until my damaged arms would be able to hold a pen again.

Mexican Standoff

Part 2: Retaliation - Original

So I lost my dinghy, I got bruised and hurt, I spent the night in the dirt, I got ripped-off and robbed. Humiliated. How deep can you fall and still not hit bottom? Once again I remember Rocky's words:

"It's not about how hard you hit, it's about how hard you can get hit and keep moving forward!"

And yes, I keep moving forward. A light breeze blows from the East. It will be a broad reach back to Isla Mujeres. Four to five hours, I guess. Slowly, like a freight train, my heavy steel ketch sets off. It takes a while until we finally reach our admittedly low cruising speed. But I am not in a hurry. About halfway to Punta Cancún I get hailed on VHF channel 16, the international emergency and hailing channel:

"Seefalke, Seefalke for Acapulco, over."

Was that really *Acapulco*? My neighbors at my anchorage at Isla Mujeres? My quarantine buddies? My friends Conny and Günter coming to my rescue?

"*Acapulco*, this is *Seefalke*, over," comes my formal reply.

S/V Acapulco coming for my rescue

We Germans are known for keeping a minimum of radio discipline even where everyone else doesn't. However, we are not as bad as the British.

"Channel 69?"

"69"

On channel 69 I learn that it was only in the morning that they read the message I sent to them last night, with my last remaining phone battery. Then they immediately set sail to come to my rescue. They figured my phone was dead and I wouldn't be able to reply. We agree to meet behind the reef of Punta Cancún, anchor there and catch up. It takes another two hours until I get there as the wind almost dies on me completely. But then my anchor, after Tropical Storm Cristobal its name is Cristo, is dropped just three boats lengths from *Acapulco.*

Rendezvous with S/V Acapulco

I jump into the warm and crystal clear water and swim over to them. We have a coffee and I tell my story, how I wanted to see my friend, how the surf destroyed my dinghy, the turtles, the jet skies, the betrayal, the humiliation. As I finish Conny is the first to speak:

"Don't let them have your motor! You need to get it back! It's not only about the motor, it's a question of honor! Don't let them get away with it!"

And Günter adds:

"But you have to do it now. Otherwise the motor will be gone for good. Time is a critical factor. Every hour counts."

At first I am not too convinced, looking at the facts that I am outnumbered badly, they are well connected with the local police, and I am not too keen to get beaten up by a Mexican beach gang. But Günter doesn't leave me a choice:

"We have lunch now. But if you have the balls I'll take you to the beach, then get a taxi and get your motor back! You will think of something, I'm sure!"

Of course I have the balls. I just have my doubts that they will be of much use during this operation.

After lunch Günter takes me to the closest beach and I get a taxi back to Playa Delfines, the scene of this morning's defeat, my personal Waterloo. I pay the taxi driver half of the agreed price and ask him to wait for me. It wouldn't take more than half an hour, one way or the other.

As I walk down the dunes I have a perfect view on the scene. Officially the beach is still closed so there are no civilians, just my enemy and me. Perfect for an honorable standoff, no collateral damages, only combatants. Just the numbers make me worry: I count eleven opponents. So I sure wouldn't win this by muscle power, also I am sure my fire power is to my disadvantage. I don't know theirs but I know mine is zero. But I have the element of surprise to my advantage and I figure they don't want too much noise among the hotels. This is where they recruit their rip-off victims. Also I am mad and pumped with adrenaline which makes me unpredictable. So all in all I think the odds are about even.

At first nobody pays attention as I descend the dunes towards the beach. But as I come closer they see and recognize me, staring at me like they've seen a ghost. Where there once was chatter, talking, and laughter, now all of a sudden there is silence and tension and all twenty-two eyes follow every single one of my movements. I try to make out that fat man, the boss. And there I see him, sitting in a camping chair in the shade of a beach pavilion. In normal no-COVID times tourists would get their sun-screen-soaked bodies treated by swift hands here. It would smell of sunscreen and oil, soap and vacation. Now it is the boss's headquarters. It smells of sweat, garlic, and chilies. I enter the chief's tent through a curtain of hostility. I walk straight up to him. I am a friend of words, I am writing essays after all. But this time I keep it short and sweet. Ok, perhaps not too sweet and admittedly neither exceedingly friendly nor particularly diplomatic:

"Hey asshole, where is my motor?"

His surprised face couldn't be more real. A great actor! I wouldn't want to play poker with him. But the game has already started. Can't bail out anymore at this point.

"Which motor, amigo?," he asks with a conciliatory smile.

"I am not your amigo and I want my motor back now, you d... sucking mother f... son of a b...," I didn't even make the effort to show a poker face.

As my Spanish is not good enough yet for impressive swearing, I spice it up with some English. Not too sure if he understands the details of the sexual abnormalities they imply for him to be involved in but I am sure he gets the point.

"I don't know anything about your motor. But let me help you, amigo."

"Has anyone seen my friend's motor?," he raises his voice so that the entire gang can hear it.

Everybody is shaking their heads in perfectly synced choreography, some with a smirk.

I am desperately outnumbered but I am mad and I am pumped. I walk up to where all his jet skies are lined up. I know that they leave them there overnight, just covered with a piece of canvas. I jump on the newest model, patting it tenderly, like a horse:

“Maybe it would help your memory if I burn down one of your jet skies?” I address the boss with my sweetest, most loving, tender voice.

“Maybe two, you never know. You took my motor but you left me my two jerrycans of gasoline. That would make a fantastic beach fire, don’t you think? Let’s meet again tomorrow, maybe you’ll remember my motor, then?”

“Tranquilo, amigo!”

“No, no tranquilo and no amigo. Let’s get this straight. We’ll be friends again as soon as I get my motor back but until then, I’m gonna torch your jetskies, one after another, night by night,” I jump off the saddle.

Despite all the tension I must smile amused as I picture his face waking up with the charred handlebar of his favorite jet ski next to him in his bed. The Godfather would be proud of me! Also I am grateful he is renting out jet skies and not horses. He smiles his most innocent smile and says:

“Hey, I now do remember your motor but we brought it to your boat, didn’t we?!”

“Well, that’s a progress but nope, you didn’t. You brought me to my boat but not my motor. Don’t try to bullshit a bullshitter!”

Then I make out the kid who was my driver this morning:

"Hey, do you remember me?"

"Yes."

"Do you remember bringing me to my boat?"

"Yes."

"Good. Now do you remember bringing my motor to my boat?"

"Hmm, you need to talk to my boss."

"I am talking to you. Do you remember bringing my motor to my boat?"

"Please! Talk to my boss!," he pleads splattering.

That is confession enough for me. I go back to the boss:

"Listen, we can do this the hard way. I torch your bar, your jet skies and I swear to all Maya gods, I will turn this beach into a battlefield as Cancún has not seen it before. I have friends who just love this stuff.," comes my convincing bluff.

"And honestly, I would enjoy this, too. (I actually really would!) Maybe I lose, but do you want to take that risk for a ridiculous 2.5 hp outboard motor? Do you really want a war? Or, we'll be all reasonable and friends again. And you will never hear from me again and you can keep ripping off gringos in peace until the end of time."

Then I decide to play the Germany card. I know that many Mexicans secretly admire Germany for the hard time we gave the Americans in WWII.

"We Germans have neither conscience nor remorse. You better not upset a German. We keep our words. We don't play. Go play with the gringos, they are easier prey anyway. Doesn't this sound appealing?"

He walks a few steps towards another closed beach bar. One of those that has swings instead of chairs. He sits on a swing and waves me to take the swing beside him. He is thinking. This is a good sign. I sit down and he offers me a beer. It is cold. I can see drops of condensate running down the can. Despite being German I don't like beer but for the sake of the negotiation I take it and open the can. So we sit a while, swinging, sipping our beers, watching out into the ocean, like year-long best buddies hanging out, having a good time. The rest of the crowd remains in respectful distance, eyeballing us. The open hostility is gone but the tension is tangible. The boss is still thinking. I see what he wants. He wants a solution that doesn't make him lose his face, and he doesn't want a big fuss about all this. Then he obviously has an idea:

"Amigo, didn't you tell us to take care of your motor and to keep it for a while until you'd be back?"

Smart guy after all. So I play along:

"Absolutely. And now I am back and would like to pick it up. And if you did what we agreed you'd do, I'd certainly consider a tip," I bluntly offer a ransom.

He smiles. I smile. Finally we are talking the same language. Two battle-experienced street-smart bullshitting field marshals preventing WWIII with a trick. The leaders of the world could learn from us. No one needs to die. All it takes are two swings, two beers, and the will to find a solution. We keep drinking our beers, swinging relaxed. We even do some small talk. He shows me photos of his wife and his kids on his smartphone. Sweet family. Maybe this fat arrogant asshole is a nice guy in his civilian life. We agree on 1,000 Pesos tip. Then he makes a phone call and two guys carry my motor and, as a bonus, my little manual drainage pump and carefully put them down on one of the beach lounges. We shake hands.

"Amigos?"

"Amigos!"

We hug. We bump our fists. The ultimate gesture of peace and understanding.

"You need to leave this beach now," an unfriendly voice barks at me from behind. I turn my head into the direction of that voice and ask the boss "Now who is this clown?"

"He is the park ranger," he replies visibly annoyed.

That was not planned. I have my doubts, though. The "park ranger's" uniform looks like he bought it in a carnival store and he clearly doesn't have the authority of an official. Also I saw him cleaning one of the jet skies earlier. My personal guess is that this guy plays the park ranger whenever one of the gringos they want to rip off makes trouble. And this time the boss was just too late to let him know the beach poker was over. He builds up in front of me and says:

"This beach is closed to the public and you have to leave now."

"I am finishing my beer and then I leave these holy grounds for good – with my motor. Relax!"

"You will need to prove to me that this is your motor!"

"If you clown can show me a valid ID I will prove to you that I am the emperor of the united kingdom of Mexico and Germany but until then, I am no longer talking to you at all."

The boss gives him a reluctant nod and he sets off and returns with a piece of paper in a plastic foil. He awkwardly presents it to me. In an unexpected, rapid move I rip it out of his hands, look at it for a glance and then I lose it. I just can't help it. I start laughing and simply cannot stop. Laughing so hard I fall off my swing and into the sand. Gasping for air I get back on my feet and sit down on my swing again. That was just the worst fake ID I have ever seen. The photo was a selfie shot, the ID No. was a row of zeros and the Mexican flag was printed the wrong way, like inverted. So, not green, white, red but red, white, green with the eagle and the snake upside down. I mean for Christ's sake, they could have put just a little more effort into this! When I finally have enough air to talk again I hand the boss 500 Pesos:

"You just lost half of your tip. I am sorry. No, I'm really not, but if you want to have my advice as an amigo: You better invest it in some better fake IDs!"

Then I stand up, take my motor and my pump and climb up those steep dunes to the parking lot. I hold the motor in my arms like a baby, damn heavy. I resist the urge to relocate that massive bastard. I won't give them that satisfaction. I also resist the urge to turn around. If they want to kill me now they have to cowardly shoot me in the back. But Mexicans are too proud to do that. Also I don't think any of them is such a good shot anyway. However, I am a bit surprised as I make it to the parking lot with no bullets in my back. The taxi is still waiting for me.

The only worries I have now are if I would remember all the details for my story until my damaged arms would be able to hold a pen again.

USA Touch and Go

As my tourist card in Mexico was about to expire soon, I was looking into options of where I could go. There was no doubt I wanted to come back to Isla Mujeres as my temporary home base but Mexican law required me to check out and check in somewhere else before I could come back to Mexico again. Everything close was still closed: Belize, Cuba, Jamaica, Guatemala, the Caymans... I still had a valid cruising license for the United States, though. Also my son was about to return to Alabama for his semester, so it would be a great opportunity to do some sailing, see my son, and renew my Mexican tourist card. So I said farewell to my friends in Isla and in Cancun and set out to sea, Alabama bound. I thought it would be a quick and easy touch and go.

I would soon know better.

At Captain's Command

A kiss. A hug. I hate goodbyes!

Without a further word I turn around and walk back to the beach that now lonely lays in the dark. Playa Tortugas, turtle beach, here in Cancun, during daytime full of families and fun, is surrounded by a net, intended to protect its guests from sharks and other deep sea critters, I suppose. Purely symbolic I am sure, because it has holes so wide that a Great White could easily slip through, but the families on the beach don't know this. It is designed to keep power boats out too, therefore it is marked with a row of red buoys that are hard to make out in the dark. My dinghy is tied to a pile that sticks out of the water maybe 60 ft outside the buoy line. My best guess is that once upon a time this pile supported a pier that no longer exists. The water is about 6 ft deep there and it was easy to swim to the beach. The street behind the beach is well lit and provides some orientation. The way back, from the light into the dark, is a totally different story, though.

And there is one more caveat: I am scared of swimming in the dark.

It is not a fear of something real, something specific. I am not afraid that dolphins start playing with my dangling balls or that a shark bites me or a jellyfish stings me. It is way more abstract, way more vague. I cannot see what is below, I cannot even see what is above, just blackness and darkness everywhere, maybe like a child feels in a dark forest. Here is the problem: as a sailor and even more so as someone who lives aboard permanently and all by himself I cannot avoid swimming in the dark every now and then. I may need to untangle a lobster trap from my rudder, or cut a fishing net out of my propeller, or sometimes I can't beach the dinghy and so I have to swim just to make it to shore. Some things just cannot wait for daylight, and as a solo sailor, lacking a crew, I cannot order someone else to do it either (it would also make me a bad captain to order my crew to do what I am afraid of doing myself).

I am scared of swimming in the dark

I remember my days in the navy, many summers ago, when at times we had to do all sorts of things that I was afraid of, such as jumping off the 35 ft high command bridge of our destroyer in full combat gear. The impact hurt badly and it took forever to make it back to the surface. Everyone was afraid, no exceptions! Us tough seamen, young, proud, invincible, now that it is more than twenty years ago, I can finally admit: we all had our pants full to the rim. But when it was our turn we all jumped without hesitating a split second. We even pretended it was fun. It was simply a question of honor, so much more powerful than fear, and there weren't even girls around to admire our courage! But one specific situation has had a special effect on me until today:

It was my time off duty, we were transiting south through the Bay of Biscay. Our ship, *Destroyer Rommel*, was part of NATO's Standing Naval Forces Atlantic (SNFL), NATO's powerful first response task force. The weather was slightly on the rough side, with 12 to 15 ft seas even our big ship would roll heavily. So much that I had to buckle up on my berth.

Destroyer Rommel of the German navy

Six hours sleep after six hours watch, phew. Combat watch system it was called, starboard watch and port watch: six hours on, six hours off, six hours on, six hours off until the end of time. I was assigned to starboard watch and then, two hours into port watch – ALARM! The alarm bell rings and from its code I know what it means before the voice comes cracking through all the speakers:

"Fire onboard! Fire onboard! All hands man battle station! Obtain battle readiness!! Fire in the stern machinery compartment! Fire in the stern machinery compartment! This is no drill! Fire on board!"

No drill, for real this time. Ok, I jump off my berth, put my clothes on in the same movement and set off towards my battle station. As a radar and radio operator my battle station was the CIC, the Combat Information Center, just behind the command bridge, towards the bow, all the way up. My berth however, was located in the stern deck for listed men, at the stern of the ship one floor below the water line. Quite a walking distance, 350 ft maybe. To avoid confusion and jamming everyone moving forward and up was supposed to do this on the starboard side, aft and down on the port side of the ship. So, I grab my gear and run. But when I reach the first ship's safety checkpoint the technical officer on watch stops me and tells me that the way to my battle station is blocked by heavy smoke. The protocol is that I check in with him and he has me join the fire fighting crew. Not good!

In the case of a fire, my assigned battle station was a good place to be: I would operate the tactical radio, inform the other ships in the task group of our situation and coordinate their support if necessary. Easy. Wouldn't get my hands dirty. But now all of a sudden I happen to be in the first line of defense. Totally not good!

The dressing crew puts me and another guy as unfortunate as me into a layer of thick leather, then an aluminum cape, then the air bottles, similar to what they use for scuba diving, then masks, a helmet and gloves. Phew, I sweat like a pig, can hardly see a thing and breathing is a challenge, too. We are the second wave, we have twelve minutes to find and fight the fire. This is how long our air is supposed to last.

The fire is in one of the machinery rooms. I think I have never been down there, in the ship's catacombs, a place of everlasting heat where the sun never shines. As we are stopped dead in the water, the ship's movements are really bad now and I feel seasickness coming up. We are waiting for the first wave to return, their mission was to find the fire, roll out the hose, mark the route to it with a guide line and, if necessary, take injured sailors back to the checkpoint. Waiting. Waiting is the worst. More waiting. I pity my two brothers of the first wave. If the fire got too bad, the captain would just say, better two than three hundred, lock the hatches and flush the compartments with CO2. Then I realize the same could happen when it was our turn. Then, finally, the round pressure hatch on the floor opens and the two guys come up, panting like marathon runners, visibly exhausted, black like chimney cleaners. Out of breath they report, nobody injured, no casualties as far as they could see, the fire is coming from the gear of the starboard engine it seems, it's extremely hot and visibility is zero, the hose is connected and rolled out, ready for the second wave. I don't want to go in there. I really don't. I have never been down there, with the smoke and in the dark I will have zero orientation in the narrow aisles. It'll be a three dimensional maze, blindfolded, in literally burning heat. No fun game. Taking the mask down means immediate disqualification, i.e. death by suffocation. The ship is rolling badly in the seas. I don't know if I am nauseous from seasickness or from sheer fear. But I know I cannot hold it much longer.

"Second wave, get ready!", the officer's voice hardly makes it to my brain.

Fear! Yes, I am afraid! I admit to myself. But don't panic, Maik, not now!! Don't panic!! I take off my mask one more time and throw up into my bag that all of us carry for that purpose. Pheew, I already feel better. I hope that gets me through the next twelve minutes. The ship is rolling heftily. I put my mask and my helmet back on and activate my air bottle. My partner and I shake hands, then we put on our over-dimensional gloves and we get ready by the floor hatch.

"Second wave, go!" and calmly but clearly audibly "Good luck, boys!", it is the voice of the STO, the Ship's Technical Officer, number three onboard, a big friendly fatherly type of guy, nothing in the world would ever get him worried.

He came down here. Wow! An NCO opens the hatch and screams at us:

"Go, go, go! Faster!!"

I promise to myself I will have a word with that asshole if and when I make it back up here, he is one of the newbies, just came from NCO training. I don't give a damn if he is of a higher rank than me. Assholes come in all ranks, and here on *Destroyer Rommel* we don't tolerate that. We are going to teach this guy the Rommel spirit, perhaps with a little physical emphasis, but first we have a fire to kill.

With difficulty we slip through that hatch and crawl down the ladder, I have that line in my hand that should guide us to the scene. I see how the hatch is closed and locked on top of us. These hatches are massive. And they are fire, water, and airtight – good for everyone on the other side. We arrive on the next floor, not too much smoke here yet, the red emergency lights throw a spooky light on our path. We open another door and climb down another companion way, open another hatch, and we are swallowed by impermeable wades of hot smoke. We cannot see shit! We are getting boiled alive in our fire protection gear. My buddy closes the hatch behind us. Slowly, hand over hand we keep following our guide line into hell's precipice. Finally we find the hose. We can see the flames now. It is not a big fire after all, but it produces so much smoke! Unbelievable!! We easily manage to extinguish it, at first we cannot believe it, we are looking for more fire sources. Then our time is up and we have to return. Still I am afraid that they wouldn't open that hatch for some reason.

'Better two than three hundred', echoes in my head. 'Bad for you if you're one of the two. Not your day, I guess.'

But as we return and knock on the hatch above our heads the same asshole that chased us in there opens it, and slowly we return back to the surface, back to life! We take the masks down, I report:

"We killed one fire, we believe it was only one source. Plenty of smoke, extreme heat."

Then I hear:

"Third wave, go!", and my partner and I hug in sheer relief:

"Happy birthday, happy birthday!"

I know, this was a long story that had little to do with *Seefalke* and her voyage, and I did not even mention that I was rewarded with two days extra vacation. But this is what I remember when I have to do something that I am afraid of, my ultimate frightening experience. And here it comes: When I need to do something I am afraid of, it helps me to get an order. Voluntarily I would have never gone into that fire. But with the order from my superior officer it was much easier, in fact, I didn't have any other choice, right?! So, even though this little episode was more than twenty years ago, I still use the very same trick: I give myself an order from a superior level, even and especially when I am by myself.

So, when I stand at Playa Tortugas in Cancun and watch into the dark, where somewhere my dinghy is tied to a derelict pile in the ocean, I hear my captain:

“Get ready to swim to the dinghy and take it back to the mothership!”

And then:

“Second wave, go! Good luck, boys!”

“Aye, cap!”

The ocean is calm. I am still wearing my heavy military boots. I won’t take them off for the swim. On land you may think they are heavy and drag you down but in fact their buoyancy is almost neutral. Once in the water, you hardly feel them but they protect you from bad cuts, especially when you swim around derelict piers and other structures that have barnacles as sharp as razor blades. I wade into the black mass until the water is hip deep. It’s warm. Not too bad. Then I start swimming into the directionI reckon my dinghy is in. Against the pitch black night sky I cannot see anything, I cannot even make out the horizon. Or anything that stands out, like a grey Zodiac for example. After an eternity I reach the buoys, but I still cannot see my dinghy. I stop and think for a short moment. I turn around. I see the street lamps, I try to remember which bearing I took when I first got here. Then I think I am too far left and head right, along the row of buoys. And yes, after a few more minutes of swimming I see the grey shape of my dinghy standing out against the black mass of water and sky. Exhausted but relieved I pull myself into the inflatable Zodiac. I take off my soaking wet clothes, crank the motor and head back to the mothership that is anchored a few hundred meters out there in the bay.

Back on board, I call my imaginary crew onto the stern deck and brief them:

"We'll weigh anchor at first daylight tomorrow. We will cross the Gulf of Mexico to Mobile, Alabama. That will be a week's passage. There is one tropical storm ahead of us in the north and one inbound further south. We will have good winds between the two and the Yucatan current is our trump, but timing is important."

Then I give my orders:

"Clear the deck! Stowe the dinghy! Check the engine! Get the ship ready to set sail first thing tomorrow morning!"

Not that I am afraid of doing all that. I am just too damn tired to do it all by myself – without the captain's command.

"Weigh Anchor at first daylight!"

A Summer Gulf Round

Crossing the Gulf of Mexico in the summer was quite a challenge. What at first glance looks like an over-dimensional circular lake turns out to be a maze of powerful currents and everlasting, almost stationary weather systems that are only interrupted by fierce squalls, tropical storms, and hurricanes. The way north was relatively easy. After I found the mighty Yucatán current it catapulted *Seefalke* and me north with breathtaking speed like riding a conveyer belt. I had trouble jumping off it before it would carry us east into the Gulf Stream. From then on it became trickier though. The gigantic, stationary high pressure zone would chaotically wobble about, producing random winds, at times at gale speed. It was exhausting and I was more than happy when I finally made it into Pensacola Bay.

Clearing into the United States became especially interesting as the customs officer's Geiger device that measures radioactivity started blinking and beeping wildly. For a moment I turned pale like a hospital wall, contemplating who the hell could have smuggled a nuclear bomb onboard. While I was thinking if I should call a lawyer or my embassy first, the dockmaster stepped up and let us know he had a medical treatment this morning, and when he returned into his office the officer's little toy calmed down, too.

After staying a few days in Pensacola I continued my voyage to Mobile, the original destination, where my son goes to college. He just rented a house with a friend and would need some help moving in. At the end I stayed in Mobile more than two weeks before I quit waiting for wind and set sail to St. Petersburg. And while I was heading south on Florida's west coast I felt like a shooting range target for hurricanes.

I learned a lot that summer 2020 in the Gulf of Mexico but the ultimate lesson that I will never forget was "You cannot always escape a hurricane."

Just in Time for Sally

I am ready.

The final countdown sequence is on. I turn the key in the ignition, wait for a short moment, then I crank the engine. The 62 hp comes to life immediately, sputtering at first but quickly the good ole diesel machine finds in its rhythm. The warning lights come off, the exhaust spits water, and after a few minutes the alternator kicks in.

"Engine ready to get underway", I report to myself.

"Cast off bow line, cast off bow and aft spring and haul them in!", I give the order to my imaginary crew that swiftly complies.

"Aye, bow line, bow spring and aft spring cast off and hauled in, Cap!"

It is in moments like these when I wish I had a crew, tired of fulfilling my own orders. Now it was only the stern line that held *Seefalke* at the dock of Ft. Myers Yacht Basin, but I cannot cast it off just yet. Half a boat length in front of me a fancy super yacht is docked, with probably three times my beam. Her name is *Snow Ghost*. I wonder how much "snow" actually is stowed on that "ghost" boat. Nomen est omen, huh?!

Stuck between a rock and a hard place

Behind me there is a shoal. Invisible, but the local diver warned me earlier not to back up any further. It was pure luck I didn't hit it when I first docked, he said. It is unmarked and just 2 ft deep. So I am literally stuck between a rock and a hard place now. No big deal I thought, cast off all lines but the stern line, use the bow thruster to turn me into position, then cast off the stern line, rudder hard starboard, engine full speed ahead and off I would go safely past that multi-million dollar floating genital extension and well clear of the shoal. But here is my dilemma:

There is current and there is wind. Both are not helpful at the moment. All week I was here there was never any wind. How often have I wished for a fresh breeze in the boiling heat! Current yes, we are in a river after all, but no wind. A few gusts during the afternoon thunderstorms, that was it.

Calm evenings at the banks of Caloosahatchee River

But now, just on time for my departure, 15 to 18 knots of wind are pushing me relentlessly against the concrete pier with those stupid huge wooden piles. I see the thunderstorm approaching. It is early today for a thunderstorm. But no big deal, I would just wait it out. An hour, maybe two tops, and I would be on my way to Key West and could still follow the falling tide down the river into the ocean. A short 140 nautical miles passage.

But my departure window is closing. I have to get going or prepare myself for a longer stay. That I don't want, not even talking about that I can hardly afford it. The girls of Ft. Myers Yacht Basin are sweet as can be and would give me any discount they could think of, but Florida is Florida, and Florida is the land of crazy docking fees. The Atlantic is busy at the moment. Hurricanes, tropical storms, depressions, and disturbances lined up like on a rope of pearls. I am not worried about the tropical storms Paulette or Rene in the center of the Atlantic, even though they are forecast to become hurricanes very soon. They would curve north and make the North Atlantic an uncomfortable place but not the Gulf.

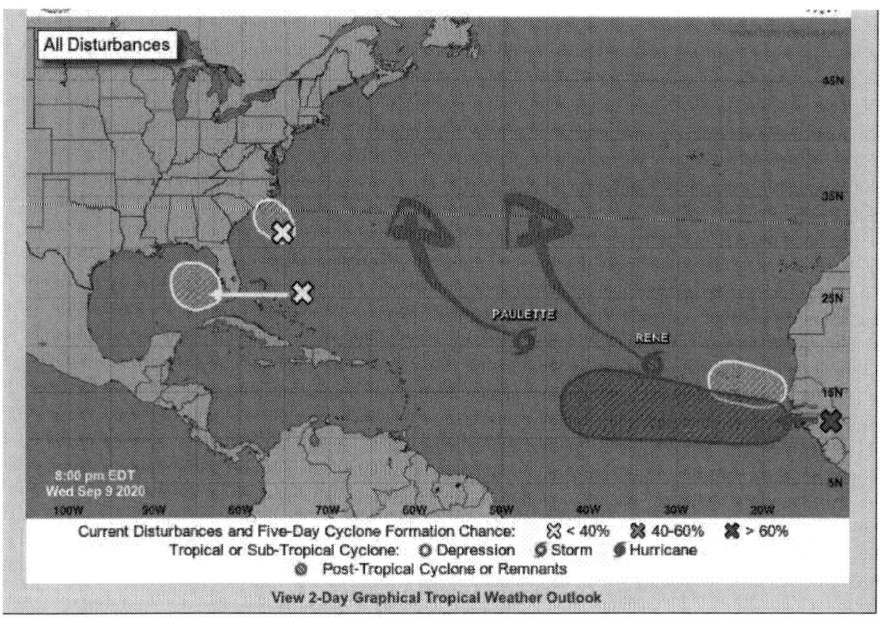

The Atlantic is busy at the moment
Credit: National Hurricane Center

The tropical depression in western Africa is still too far to worry about, it has the potential to delay or divert my onward travels, yes, but nothing to worry about at this time. But there is this stupid little tropical disturbance. It just popped up east of the Bahamas and the NHC, the National Hurricane Center (the US National Hurricane Center in Miami is the coordinator for the hurricane forecast in the Atlantic) did not give it much chance of development. It would move right into my path though. Reason enough to study the detailed discussion for this weather system. "Discussion" is what the meteorologists call the document that describes how they come to their forecast conclusion. It is usually a two page document in which the different factors that are supposed to have influence on the weather system in question are weighed and evaluated. I already read many of those discussions and I slowly start to be able to decipher their hieroglyphic language.

The guy who wrote this discussion was sure it would get uncomfortable in the eastern Gulf very soon even though the leading weather models wouldn't support his conclusion. This is why he downrated the "probability of development". I checked the GFS (Global Forecast System) and also the ECMWF (European Centre for Medium-Range Weather Forecast) models before and yes, he was right, they promised light to moderate northerly to easterly winds that I planned on utilizing to slowly take me to Key West. It actually looked more like light wind sailing than storm sailing conditions. But the guy who wrote that discussion, I think his name was Martinez, had a gut feeling this would become something bigger very soon, and if I have learned anything in my sailing career it's that the gut feeling of an experienced meteorologist is worth more than thousand computer models.

So, long story short, I wanted to get out of here and be in Key West before that tropical disturbance would disturb me too much. If I would miss the tide it would take me forever to reach the mouth of the mighty Caloosahatchee River and consequently, I would miss the moderate breeze that would move southwards with me, and as a result, all my route planning would be nil and void. Then I would be sitting ducks for that weather to come and get me. This is just for you to understand that I could not wait forever and that if I would not depart within the next few hours I would be tied to this dock for at least another week.

On the other hand, my bow thruster is not powerful enough to push my thirteen tons against 15 to 18 knots of onshore wind and the tidal river current would push me right into that super yacht. (Spring line maneuvers are difficult, almost impossible with my full keel boat.) I am not worried about my boat, *Seefalke* is made from steel and she would easily win a tête-à-tête with *Snow Ghost*. Only I am sure the owner would not appreciate *Seefalke's* orange signature on her high gloss polished hull. I also cannot back out because of the shoal right behind me. I must think of my own quote "Patience is the captain's most important quality. It's the lack of patience that sink ships." Being on a schedule is deadly, it makes you set sail when you know you shouldn't. It makes you lie to yourself.

"Yes, I can take that shortcut!", and bang, you run aground. "Yes, my motor is strong enough to maneuver out of this narrow marina at these winds!", and bang, you drift full speed ahead into the boat just docked next to you. "Yes, I should reef now but I want to get there before nightfall!", and bang, your sail is shredded to pieces. Been there, done that, bought the t-shirt.

Impatience at sea is deadly. And I know it. And now I am stuck here with three options:

1. I could try the maneuver and if I fail spend the rest of my life working off the damage I would do to that super yacht. (Ok, I am actually insured, but still...)

2. I could wait a few more hours, run straight into that tropical depression and find out in person if the NHC meteorologist's gut or the computer weather models were right.

3. I could just turn off the engine, call it a day, go to the counter, pay another 500 USD and stay here for another week.

And while I am evaluating my options, I notice that the wind calms down. It's not 15 to 18 knots anymore but just 12 to 15 now. And once in a while it even goes below ten knots, that my bow thruster can handle. I order my imaginary stern deck crew to double the fenders and put the stern line on slip. I order that same crew to populate the foredeck and get the big boat hook ready to help push us off. I tell my virtual machine room crew to go slow speed ahead. Then the helmsman gets the order to put the rudder hard starboard. We are all ready for the next break in the gusts, it would just take one word of the captain and the maneuver would begin. Waiting. 15 knots, 17, 14, 15 again. Phew... the stern line groans under the load. Then 12 knots, 10, 8, 9...

"Now!!"

"Push off the bow to starboard, bow thruster full starboard, engine half speed ahead!"

I push the engine lever forward, hit the starboard button of the bow thruster. The bow invisibly slowly starts turning, arrrgh. The manual says max. two minutes per hour to avoid overheating. So after one minute I jump on the foredeck, grab the boat hook and start pushing. Slowly the bowsprit starts pointing outwards. But not enough yet.

Back in the cockpit I hit the bow thruster again. But the wind is picking up. Eighteen knots again. No way!

“Abort maneuver!”, I sigh.

Sluggishly *Seefalke* moves back to her starting position. After 10 minutes, another break in the gusts, another attempt. This time the bow starts moving, I keep hitting the bow thruster, I don’t want to lose the momentum. It smells burnt, but it’s now or never!

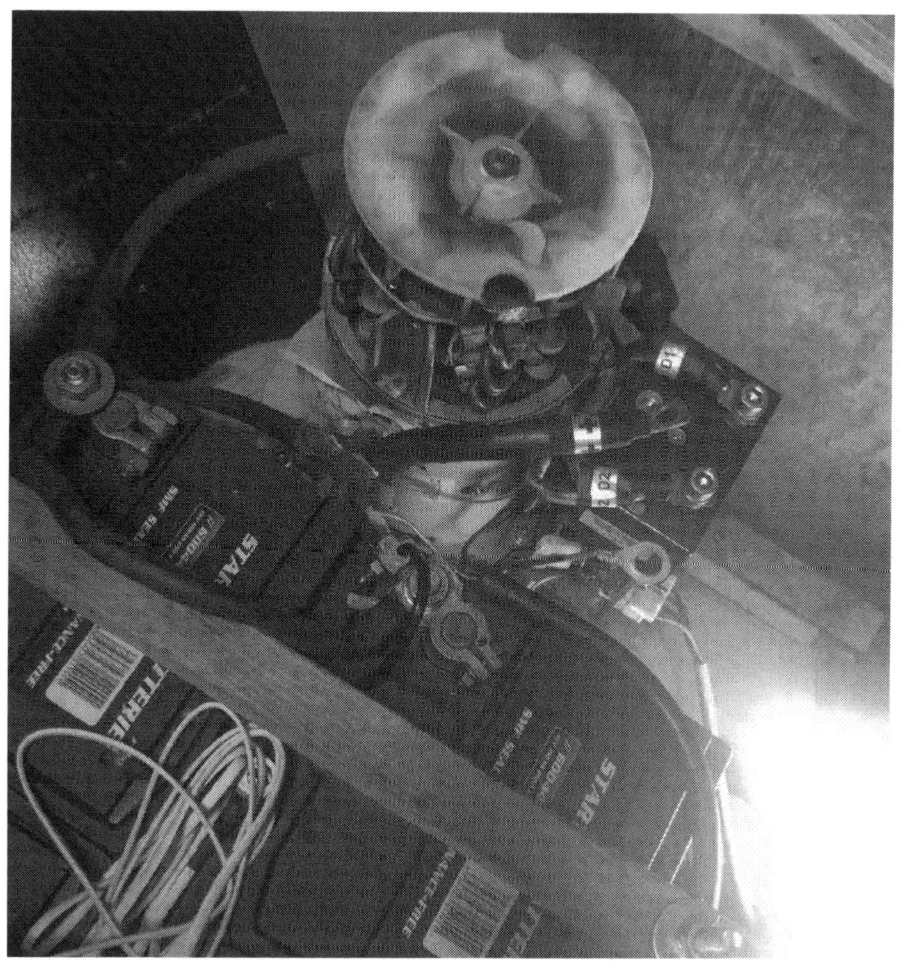

The bow thruster smells burnt, but it’s now or never

Finally the bow thruster quits on me, wads of smoke are blocking my view to the bow hatch. I run onto the foredeck, give the boat her final push, run back to the stern deck, haul in the stern line, jump into the cockpit and crank the engine to full speed ahead. Eventually my ole steel battleship gains speed, we come well clear of that super yacht and finally are on our way.

Finally, we are on our way

"Clear the deck!", is my last order to my virtual crew before I go below to check on my poor bow thruster.

It doesn't smell good, that's a fact. But it got us out of here and that is the main thing. I switch off the bow thruster main, I will take care of it later. As we, I like to refer to *Seefalke* and me as "us", make way down the mighty Caloosahatchee River I reluctantly collect the fenders and stow them, coil up the docking lines and get the deck ready for whatever it will be that is awaiting us out there. Will it be the relaxed sail that GFS, the Global Forecast System, the leading US weather model is promising or will it be as rough as the NHC meteorologist feels in his guts? The most interesting is that even the European weather model ECMWF (European Centre for Medium-Range Weather Forecasts) is in a very rare intimate accord with its American counterpart. And still the NHC guy feels differently.

The system is still over the Bahamas and it sure will take two days to make it here but there is a little detail that alerts me. The "disturbance" had been upgraded to a "tropical depression" after just two days and in parentheses the cute name "Sally" appeared. So they already reserved a name for this system. That fast?? This means Martinez is worried and I should be, too. I still have internet and I download a set of GRIB files (Gridded Binary weather files) for both GFS and ECMWF models and both show the finest sailing weather all the way from today (Thursday) till the beginning of next week and for my complete route. I am confused. But I know I don't have a lot of time to waste.

Skyline of Marco Island

View to the West

View to the East

When I finally reach the Gulf, dolphins are welcoming me as they always do. The sunset is gorgeous and the night comfortable with a light breeze. Just as the weather forecast promised. At sunrise I pass the distinct skyline of Marco Island, the breeze dies and I turn on the engine to help our progress. That's something I do very rarely, I rather enjoy the slowness and wait for the wind than breaking the quietude and peacefulness with that roar and stink of the diesel.

But this time, I just want to make it to Key West before Sally does. In the early afternoon black clouds come up from the East, the sky sparkling and twinkling from lightning, whereas the west grants me another awesome sunset. I prefer to not look to the East too much. Too scary.

One thunderstorm passes my stern, I barely escape its gust front with those dreadful fringes that easily can turn into water spouts as my VHF radio starts to crackle:

"Securité, securité, securité, this is the United States Coast Guard sector Key West, Florida... heavy thunderstorms... local gusts up to 50 knots... locally high waves... local risk of waterspouts... all mariners are requested to seek safe harbor immediately... this is the United States Coast Guard. Out."

Holy Moly! The US Coast Guard is not easily impressed. If they make an announcement like that they have a reason. But no safe harbor close to me, to my east it is just the vast Everglades in 60 nautical miles and it is just another 60 nautical miles to Key West. So I have no choice than to continue my track as I find myself surrounded by fierce thunderstorms at nightfall. I replace my medium genoa with my small one made of heavy fabric and tie a reef in the main. The gusts beautifully accelerate my heavy steel ship and we cut through the waves like a hot knife through butter.

We cut through the seas like a hot knife through butter

The gusts are not too bad, 25 maybe 28 knots, easily manageable but the lightnings start to concern me. I start counting the time, calculating the distance, estimating the direction, trying to figure the thunderstorms' movements, making course adjustments to avoid them.

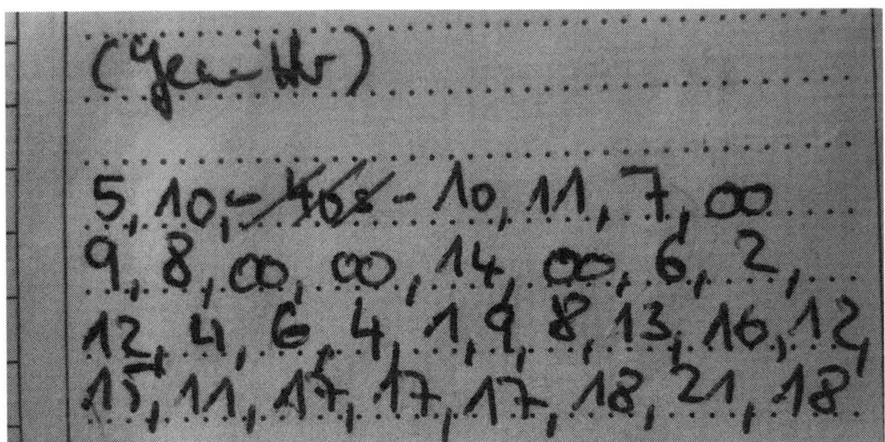

Lightning distances in nautical miles

But all in all I feel pretty helpless and finally decide to just steer the course that takes me to Key West the fastest. This is where my good friends from *S/V Off the Grid* are waiting for me.

S/V Off the Grid welcomes me

After a sleepless night I finally have a visual of Mud Key in the morning. The waves build up, but nothing too worrying yet, just high enough to see those thousands of lobster traps just in the very last moment. How many can there be, really?!! A minefield!! I am relieved when I finally reach the approach channel as hell breaks loose. The sky turns pitch black dark and the torrential rain takes away all visibility. I finally drop my heavy duty Bruce anchor, whose name is Cristo (after I rode out Tropical Storm Cristobal in Mexico earlier in the season, I promised to name it) just outside the channel and decide to wait it out right here. Three hours later, when there is a short break in the rain, I continue to my anchorage, set plenty of chain, and think to myself:

"Just in time!"

Torrential rain takes away all visibility

I admire the Coast Guard radio operator. She remains cool when all the distress calls are coming in, does her best to calm people down. And I keep my fingers crossed for all the poor souls out there fighting for their lives. Nothing I can do from here. I hear that a Coast Guard officer who was sent to rescue the crew of a small sailboat fell off the helicopter and is now fighting for his own life, too, in 9 ft seas. Nothing I can do.

This sneaky Sally bitch! Just in time.

Back in Isla

After all the storms I dodged and weathered in the Gulf I had the illusion that when I was back on Isla Mujeres this would be over. It had been 15 years since the last hurricane, hurricane Wilma, so statistically Isla can be considered safe.

Just sometimes statistics bite you in the ass.

Tied to a Rope of Sand

Something is wrong

A beautiful scene. The boat is heeling in the evening breeze. The mainsail is hauled tight, and all this in front of a romantic sunset. But something is wrong.

No spray is flying, no bow is cutting through the waves, no whooshing, no splashes – no movement at all. No sound. A still. Surreal.

I am standing in knee-deep water and looking at *Seefalke*, my 40-foot steel ketch, stranded like a whale. It is day two. She looks sad. But also a bit defiant, as if she is trying to say:

"Ok, we lost this battle but we will win the war!"

While *Seefalke's* battle cry dies away over the Bahia of Isla Mujeres at the very eastern tip of Yucatán Peninsula in Mexico, I am trying to remember how we got into this unfortunate position: a story of unlucky circumstances. No, I want to be honest, it is a story of negligence and poor seamanship.

Gamma was born three days ago. Gamma is not only the third letter of the Greek alphabet but also the twenty-fourth named storm of this very active season 2020. With 60 knots maximum sustained winds near hurricane force tropical storm Gamma is now approaching the Yucatán peninsula. The intense hurricane season 2020 drained the regular names in no time hence we are learning the Greek alphabet now. I know the drill. By now I know the drill. Tropical storms cannot worry me anymore. Or as the Dalai Lama had said in one of his famous poems

"It is called calm and it cost me many storms."

I weathered Cristobal here in Isla Mujeres, I slipped through the remnants of Gonzalo and mature Hanna in the Gulf of Mexico on my way to Mobile, Alabama, I dodged Marco and Laura on Florida's west coast, weathered adolescent Sally in Key West. And all this just in one season. I have seen many storms. I am calm.

The holding here in the Bahia is notorious. I veer more chain, 150 ft at the end at just 8 ft of water depth. I crank the engine up to 2,000 rpm astern. The water is fizzing and whirling but we don't move a hair. This is how I like it. Perfect! Then I set my second anchor, at an angle of 50 to 60 degrees from the first, with 60 ft of ½ inch chain and 60 ft lead line. 2,000 rpm astern until we stop moving. What is the equivalent in wind of 2,000 rpm? I don't know, but I know if anything is going to break our neck it will be the gusts, not the sustained wind. This was the setup that safely brought me through Cristobal. Still I put on my goggles and dive both anchors, it looks good! Doubts creep over me when I realize, I am anchored exactly in the center of the dragging during tropical storm Cristobal. My friends from *S/V Off the Grid* dragged here, and *S/V Maverick, S/V Sukha* and in another storm earlier *S/V Acapulco.* All experienced captains with good anchors, and plenty of chain. I know the holding, two cables further east is much better. But then I think about the hassle of hauling in the second anchor manually, then the main anchor, then relocating and dropping the two anchors again, then driving them in and diving them. Two hours work for sure. Pheew, no, too lazy. So I decide my Bruce and my Delta with plenty of chain will do. Even here. At this notorious holding. I clear the deck and tie everything that could possibly fly away. I secure my dinghy with another line and batten down the hatches.

I am ready! Gamma may come!! Bring it on!!!

And Gamma comes. At nightfall the wind is picking up. It is dangerously howling in the stays and shrouds: the familiar soundtrack of the storm. The halyards are loudly beating against the mast. I have to tie them off but the rain is torrential. The desire to go out there is low, very low, none existent. Which is still an understatement. But the continuous clanking is driving me nuts! So, finally I take off all my clothes and naked as a jaybird I crawl through that little hatch. I am soaked before I fully make it out there. The rain shoots horizontally, it feels like hail, stinging hurtfully like someone keeps throwing gravel at me. Or darts. Instinctively I keep my crotch in lee when I work my way to the mast. It is cold out here so my crown jewelry doesn't make a big target but better safe than sorry. Out here it is so deafeningly loud I can't hear the clanking no more. I tie the halyards to the sea fence and hope that does the trick. Then I slip through that little hatch back into my storm shelter. Awww, this feels good! While I am rubbing myself down with a towel, I listen to the sound of the storm, the clanking stopped.

Shortly before midnight the wind is steadily in its thirties, with gusts in the forties. The gusts hit like slaps in the face. They don't come head on. They strike from the side like Thor's hammer. They make *Seefalke* heel and accelerate until the chain stops her rudely and she straightens up again, waiting for the next burst. On the iPad in my nav corner I see the plotter data, received by WiFi, fancy. And very practical. So I don't have to go out there in the rain. The anchor alert is set but *Seefalke* moves in a perfect textbook swing. No dragging, yet.

I try to sleep a little until a voice on the radio is waking me up. It is a big catamaran calling the port captain, asking for tow assistance. I look out of my portholes and try to make out that boat. But the night is impenetrable with torrential rain coming down as if there is no tomorrow. The repeated calls remain unanswered, the Port Captain is long asleep. At first the voice is full of confidence, then panic takes over, then resignation. Finally I decide to call them knowing I cannot even offer my assistance in these conditions but maybe I can calm them down a bit. It turns out they dragged and are sitting in the mangroves now. Nothing they can do but wait. The good news is they cannot drag any further. Then my friends from *S/V Bullseye* start dragging right towards me. I see them desperately fighting with their anchor chain on the foredeck. In the last moment they get their little motor fired up and struggle to return to their anchorage. It is a challenge to fight the storm with just 12 hp, but eventually this brave crew succeeds. The gusts are close to 50 knots now. Then I see movement on my plotter. We have clearly moved 20 ft where we shouldn't. But we have stopped again. It seems the anchor has found a new holding point. Still I am alert. I crank the engine. Just in case. First I think the engine wouldn't start because I cannot hear it. But then I check the rev meter and I see it is running just fine. Just the howling of the wind drowns out everything. A few more terrible gusts go through and I start to relax. In the next moment a deep groaning is jolting the ship and I see how *Seefalke* is taking a 60 degree angle to the wind, the typical dragging position. I put the engine in gear to get prepared to re-anchor. But after a few seconds the motor dies. I don't hear it but I see the warning lights come on on my panel and the rev meter needle rests at zero.

The worst case scenario!

It takes me only a fraction of a second to understand what this means. We must have caught something in the propeller. That's it. We are doomed. Nothing I can do but release the ignition and brace for the impact when we will hit the sandbar. Demoted from captain to spectator in the blink of an eye. But there is some good news, too. There is no other boat downwind between me and the sandbar and the beaching is soft and gentle. As soft and gentle as it gets with the choppy seas and forty-five knots of gusty winds.

As soon as we come to a temporary halt, I grab my goggles, my sailor's knife, and my gloves and jump into the water. If I can get those lines off the propeller quickly, I still might have a chance to come free by my own power. At first I am a bit surprised the water is only shoulder deep, but sure, my draft is 5 ft and we just ran aground. All logical. I am in the lee of *Seefalke* where at least she gives me some protection from the moved seas. Then I slide underneath the boat. I come back up instantaneously. I hit my head badly and I cannot see a thing in the water with all the sand stirred up. I take off my goggles, I have to feel my way to the propeller. I guess I take the gloves off now, too.

Demoted from captain to spectator

It is still pitch black dark when I slide back underneath the boat, just hoping I wouldn't get wedged or crushed. Wouldn't be a nice way to die. Not a good feeling with thirteen tons wildly moving over my head with nowhere to escape. Not good at all. But my only chance. Who wants to live forever anyway? I feel the lines, they are not melted, not even jammed. I may get them out by just untwisting them. In the meantime I see the boat slowly shuffling herself further up the sandbar. She heels over a lot.

After an eternity I get the first line off and I take a break. Blood is running down my fingers, hands and arms but I cannot feel the pain. Yet I know I will for the next few days. Barnacles cut deep into the flesh and saltwater doubles the fun. My head must be bruised and swollen, but I don't care. I just need to get these lines out. A few more dives and I will have made it. But the last bit I need to cut nevertheless. It turns out it is hard to re-find the cutting notch on the line. The line is too good (or my knife too bad) to cut it in one shot. After 45 minutes I report to myself "propeller clear". But it is too late. The storm has pushed us too far onto the sandbar. No way I can make it back with only my motor.

The sun should have risen but it seems to be waiting for the storm to end, too. It's way after sunrise but still pretty dark. Back in the boat, from my elevated position, I see the reef very close, and downwind. Too close. If we keep moving we will get pushed over the sandbar and right into the rocks. The wind is calming down a bit to steady thirty knots but I am still concerned. Ahead of us, just twenty meters away there is a half-submerged wreck. I think it was hurricane Wilma that put it there. On normal days it is a snorkeling paradise for tourists. I decide that today it will be my mooring. So I haul in my primary anchor until only twenty meters of chain are out. Then I go back into the water, carry the anchor a few meters, until the chain becomes too heavy, then I carry the chain towards the anchor, then I carry the anchor a bit further. The anchor and the chain are just too heavy to move them all at once.

It is an arduous work, in the storm, in the seas, in the current that now has become significant. It takes me almost an hour to reach the wreck. An hour for twenty meters! It is all rusted, with sharp edges and covered in barnacles. I expected that, that's why I have my shoes on. I find a corner in which I wedge the anchor. At least now I won't go anywhere. Phew... First time in many hours I relax. Slowly I trudge back to the boat. While I am trying to get dry and warmed up I see that *S/V Dodue*, the wooden ketch of my friend Santiago stranded, too, and she is coming dangerously close!

The wreck becomes my mooring

Tête-a-tête with S/V Dodue

Santiago comes over, in his bright yellow raincoat and asks if I have some coffee for him. So I brew some for the two of us. Santiago is Columbian. He and his Swiss girlfriend Alicia sail the world together but on their two boats. A great concept! Now Alicia is in Switzerland to give sailing lessons on Lake Geneva and Santiago takes care of both boats. It is tough to take care of one boat all by yourself, but two boats in conditions like this, almost impossible. I admire him. He has guts! And enough smoke, too. He tells me that he slept on Alicia's boat during the storm and that he was totally shocked when he got up and realized the other boat was gone. And how happy he was to find it on this sandbar and not in Cancún or on the rocks or never. So, despite the unfortunate circumstances he is in a pretty good mood. And he is right! It could have come worse.

The catamaran that called for help in the night was sitting all the way in the mangroves, buried in half a meter of sand and mud. They will sure have some trouble to get out of there! After we have our coffee, I lay down and try to get some sleep. I can hardly keep myself upright. But after one hour I get up again and hail the Port Captain on the radio. Surprisingly enough he responds to my call but tells me I need to call the coast guard on the phone and he gives me their number. So I call the coast guard, but they are not happy to come out. Are people in danger? No, no people are in danger, just boats. No, they don't come out for boats. Later they call me back and let me know they are coming now with two rescue swimmers and a big RIB I should have everything ready. Maybe the Port Captain had a word with them?

An hour later I see their boat, and a little later I see two men in the water heading my way with a tow line. We make the connection and I drop more anchor chain so that we have room to move. But then such disappointment! The commander of the RIB orders to abort the mission. The gusts were too dangerous and people and equipment were at risk. Really?? I had eight sailboat crews standing by in their dinghies ready to jump in without a second thought but the professional coast guard is scared of thirty knot gusts? I hope I will never get into real trouble here. Then I have to fill in tons of paperwork and make a video statement that I refuse to be rescued and wish to remain onboard. Quite a lot of hassle for no help.

Then all my friends show up, one after another. Quite a view! This feels good!! At the end we have eight dinghies between 5 and 60 hp. Two of them are YouTube camera crews though, but when their camera batteries die they join the crowd. One pulling my mast down to heel me, the rest trying to pull me back into the channel. But no way. The wind had shifted. On the one side this is good. I hoisted my mainsail and the wind, still strong, helps to heel us. But it is also now pushing the water out of the bay. Even high water cannot compensate for that.

Heeling at any cost

I need more power! But first I need some rest. The next day I call my friend Martin, captain of *NEMO*, a glass bottom boat that looks like a submarine. It is bright red and has a friendly face. He has a friend with a 300 hp tourist boat that usually takes tourists out to the best diving grounds. That could work! An hour later they are here. And yes, we move the boat just about 6 ft but not an inch further. We understand that we will have to wait for high water which will be at 2234hrs tonight. So we abort again and reschedule for 2130hrs.

In the meantime I realize in shock that I left the head porthole open and a lot of water had come in while we were heeling the boat. Damnit!! Nobody else's ass I can kick for this but mine!! I don't realize yet that it will be over 150 gallons of water that I took on. It will destroy most of my provisions, most of my paints and some of my electronics.

Then I try to pull the boat forward towards my anchor using my windlass. "Kedging" this is called. But no way. I will have to wait for high water. The afternoon passes in slow motion. I feel like living on a climbing wall with *Seefalke* laying on her side. Every movement in the boat becomes a climbing challenge. It almost looks like one of these houses they sometimes have in amusement parks where everything is upside down.

Living on a climbing wall

At 2100hrs we start the next attempt. The water is 10 inch higher now. Not much but maybe that will do the trick. I receive a text message from Martin, they are coming with 400 hp now. Good! He is great!

Liam from Australia is there with his 60 hp RIB and Ken from the US is back, too. German from Argentina and Fahrettin from Turkey and Philippe from France. It's good to have friends! Liam takes the halyard again and Martin and Marcelo with their heavy power boat take the tow line. At first nothing moves at all. We are sitting like cast in stone. Then Liam pulls us over just a hair more (I am a bit worried about my rigging and more water in the boat but this is our only chance.) and all of a sudden we glide through the sand like my hull is greased with Vaseline. I give Liam the signal to stop pulling and we are coming upright again. We are afloat!! Only now I have to hurry to take my sail down or I will bump into my rescue boat. I hear cheering from the boats in the anchorage:

"Hurrayyy!!! Hurrayyy!!! Yippieh!!!"

But then my motor won't crank. I sense it got some water or too much sand. So I ask the tug to pull me into a marina in the lagoon. Shortly before we arrive my motor finally cranks, spitting and stuttering at first but then purring smoothly as a cat and I can do the docking maneuver under my own power. Man, that feels good! My good ole Peugeot tractor motor, competently marinized by Vetus obviously is hard to kill!

Safely docked

It is midnight when *Seefalke* is finally safely docked and our little land trip is over. Martin tells me we might get another "little wind" in a few days.

Nobody had an idea that that little wind would be known as cat 4 hurricane Delta in the morning.

Hurricane Delta

Isla Mujeres and the Yucatán Peninsula are not hit very often by hurricanes or tropical storms. For being inside the hurricane belt the area is as hurricane safe as it gets. At least statistically. The last hurricane was hurricane Wilma in 2005 and before that in 1988. But it is the nature of statistics that sometimes they turn around and bite you in the butt. And so the "little wind" that my friend Martin was talking about turned into a category four hurricane just four days after we were hit by tropical storm Gamma, and just another two weeks later hurricane Zeta paid us a visit. Three major storms in three weeks after no hurricane in 15 years, this is why averages suck. But what exactly is a category four hurricane?

A category four hurricane is a major hurricane with top sustained wind speeds around 115 knots. This is impossible to imagine unless you have already seen it and survived to tell the story. However, in their general description the National Hurricane Center in Miami leaves no doubt what category four means:

"Catastrophic damage will occur. Well-built framed homes can sustain severe damage... Most trees will be snapped or uprooted and power poles downed... Power outages will last weeks to possibly months. Most of the area will be uninhabitable for weeks or months."

And their recent forecast bulletin for hurricane Delta reads like a horror thriller:

"... extremely dangerous category four hurricane Delta heading toward the northeastern coast of the Yucatan Peninsula ... expected to bring life-threatening storm surge and extreme winds ... catastrophic wind damage is expected within portions of the northern Yucatan Peninsula of Mexico beginning tonight. All preparations to protect life and property should be rushed to completion."

The northeastern coast of Yucatán Peninsula, this is exactly where we were.

I was scared.

Hailing Heaven

All of a sudden it is calm.

No movement. Not the slightest breeze. Not the usual cacophony of Reggaeton music, barking dogs, and roaring power boats. Even the birds stopped chirping.

The world is holding its breath.

This happened so suddenly, like someone pulled the plug in the dance club. Subconsciously I want to stick my fingers in my ears to prevent my eardrums imploding from this deafening sound of silence. After the hustle and bustle of the morning this abrupt hush is eerie. Am I the only soul left on this planet? Has a deadly virus come over us and killed everyone else? Or an alien invasion? The good news is it is not a virus (ok, not only), and it is not an alien invasion either. The bad news, however, is that it is a storm. It is the calm before the storm. To be precise, the calm before a category four hurricane. So if now is not the time to get shit scared, when else?

We, this is *S/V Seefalke* and I, are docked in the lagoon of Isla Mujeres, still licking our wounds from tropical storm Gamma, that swept over us just three days ago, pushing us on a sandbar. The NHC says:

"All preparations to protect life and property should be rushed to completion."

And yes, we are rushing to complete our preparations to protect life and property. Because we were not granted much heads-up. Yesterday at this time we were still expecting a category one hurricane passing us 300 miles to the East. Only in the evening, after the first hurricane hunter aircraft investigated the storm, we learned that it was upgraded to a cat-4 aiming right at us, becoming the fastest intensifying Atlantic cyclone in 15 years. In the night we were all hoping the trajectory would move somewhere else. Hope dies last. And we all woke up to a red alert hurricane warning this morning. The trajectory was confirmed. I guess we better batten down the hatches now.

The lagoon that I am docked in is Makax Lagoon. It is the only hurricane hole in the area. And a good one, too. In 2005 during hurricane Wilma, the last hurricane to hit Isla Mujeres, boats in the lagoon were the only ones still afloat after the storm whereas Cancún, just a few miles away, suffered immense damage. So no wonder boats and ships from all over the place seek shelter now in the mangroves and in the marinas of the lagoon as long as their draft allows. Even the Ultramar passenger ferries come here. In the afternoon there is an endless line of boats passing through the narrow channel that connects the lagoon with the Bahia and the Caribbean. Even though it has been 15 years since the last hurricane, everyone knows the drill and the preparations follow a strict choreography:

The Port Captain closes the ports, ferry traffic is suspended. "Ley Seca" is activated, which means alcohol sale is prohibited. Shelters are opened. Exposed areas are evacuated. Then stores and supermarkets close and everybody needs to go home. Police and navy soldiers make sure nobody is on the streets. Later the big ferries block the entrance to the lagoon to mitigate storm surge. The lagoon is bustling. Boats are being anchored, tied up to the mangroves and docks, additional lines are being brought out until every boat looks like a fly in a spiderweb. Then the boats are stripped down, sails and booms, biminis and dodgers, solar panels and wind generators, everything that creates unnecessary windage goes inside. My estimate is 500 to 600 boats are now seeking shelter in the lagoon. It almost feels like you can walk across jumping from boat to boat. But am I ready? Can you ever get ready for a category four hurricane at all? I am going through my checklist again and again. And again and again I see something else that I have not seen before. A jerry can on deck for example, or a boathook that was not lashed yet. In the past I would ask myself

"Can wind tear this off?", and mostly the answer would be:

"No. Wind cannot tear this off."

But then I remember the footage of that freight train in Louisiana, tipped over by hurricane Laura. So, I slightly adjusted that question to:

"Can something that can tip over a freight train tear this off?", and now the answer is:

"Yes!!", and it slowly sinks in that nothing is safe from something that can tip over a freight train. Nothing.

I think my boat is ready. As ready as it gets. The biggest difference between a tropical storm and a hurricane is that if you do everything right in a tropical storm, you will survive it. In a hurricane you can do everything right and still not survive. Luck is a big factor. Now the waiting begins. The waiting is the worst. Too much time to think.

Every thought worries and scares me more. I am not ashamed to say I am afraid. I am shit scared, with my pants full to the rim.

I look at the wooden dock again that I am tied to. On the first glance it looks massive, but it looks fragile compared to the dock at Palafox Pier Marina in Pensacola, Florida that got annihilated during hurricane Sally. The slip that I used a few months ago when I was there, simply does not exist anymore. Also I remember footage from Orange Beach, Alabama, that I passed a few months ago. Docks similar to mine were simply erased, including the boats tied up to them. So, my head is bustling with what-if-scenarios:

What if the cleats on the dock come off? What if the poles collapse? What if the storm surge lets the water level rise over the pier? What if the entire pier gets torn to pieces? What if the neighbouring dock comes adrift and plays wrecking ball?

I don't trust my dock. The locals can say what they want. I drop my anchor. Just in case. And I bring out my stern anchor, too. Just in case.

Category four means wind speeds of up to 135 knots. In other words hundred thirty-five!! "Catastrophic wind damage" the National Hurricane Center's forecast echoes in my head. Ok, we are in a hurricane hole, protected by mangroves and higher grounds toward the East where the main blow will be coming from but what will be our number? How much of the catastrophic winds will we see? Will the docks withstand these enormous forces? The locals are confident. They tie up their boats and go home. They have survived Wilma and in their eyes it cannot get any worse. Many cruisers leave their boats too and go into a hotel for the night, or get drunk or stoned or both.

I can't. I can't leave my boat. Not now. I pack my grab-bag just in case but I have trouble imagining what would have to happen for me to use it. It would break my heart to abandon my boat in the hour of need. And – a little superstitious – she could do the same to me one day.

More waiting. It is pure torture. Now bring it on already! I have made my move, and the opponent is taking it slow. A mind war. I am sure it is not giving it justice but I am feeling what I imagine that the WWI soldiers felt in their trenches waiting for the assault.

Still not the slightest air movement. The silence is overwhelming. I am exhausted but there is no way I can sleep now. So, I am preparing an excel sheet to record wind speeds, wind direction, and pressure every half hour. At least this keeps me busy. Before nightfall I check the docking lines and the deck one more time. Looking good.

Finally the wind is picking up. In normal days not enough to be worth mentioning. Sustained winds are around ten knots now, gusts around eighteen knots. Hope is coming up: Maybe we get spared after all? The system is strong but relatively small and fast moving, so maybe it tacked in the last moment? Sometimes hurricanes do the weirdest things.

But then, all of a sudden, long after midnight, the barometer starts falling: 1010 hPa, 1005 hPa, passing 1000 hPa. The sustained winds are surprisingly low, but relentless gusts unload their explosive charges like bombs. The noise is deafening. The docking lines creak and groan, the stays and shrouds scream and howl. The movements are brutal now, every gust makes *Seefalke* list and shiver when the wind hits the resonance frequency of the rigging. The lightning show is spectacular, for unbroken moments at a time it is bright as day while in my steel-sheltered cabin-cage I get beaten and shaken like riding the Niagara in a barrel. I remember what the locals said and try to relax. Evert, my friend in Switzerland, is texting me and provides me with updated weather information. That helps. My mom calls with the last cell service we have. That helps, too. Then the phone is dead.

We pass 995 hPa, the barometer is in free and bottomless fall now, the gusts are deep in the 50-knots range. I doubt that we will be able to survive twice this or even more. How much more can we take? How much longer will it last? Around 0500hrs in the morning we pass 985 hPa, the wind is now gusting up to 70 knots. On the other side of the lagoon a headsail comes loose from one of the sailboats in the mangroves. Slapping in the wind it bangs like machine gun fire. Not much they can do against it now, if they are even onboard.

Then a bang that makes my blood freeze and my eardrums burst, like a hand grenade explosion in direct vicinity. A lightning strike maybe? I have to get out and check on it. The rain is torrential and I can hardly keep my eyes open against the wind and the rain that feels like needles. Then I see it. One of the docking lines snapped. But there are two more, so we are ok. I am also relieved it was the line and not the cleat or the dock. Pheeeww... I also see that the water level rose by almost one meter in the last hour. I just hope that the eye will pass soon, making the wind shift and drain the lagoon again. If not, we will get a completely different problem soon. Completely soaked, I crawl back into my confined bunker of steel. And while I am rubbing myself dry, *Seefalke* is jerking and yanking like a rodeo bull. Poor girl!

Then, in the heat of the fight with the elements, the radio starts cracking, first some upset screams mixed with static, full of panic and fear, I cannot understand a word. Then a fatherly voice:

"Keep calm, boys! We are all in this together, amigos!", then another voice, stumbling that two boats just got loose and are headed for the mangroves.

All radio discipline is gone to hell. And then, in a break of all this chaotic radio chatter, a calm but trembling voice starts praying:

"Padre nuestro que estás en el cielo…", obviously hailing heaven on VHF channel 16 in sheer despair.

The screams on the radio, this man's prayer and the relentless soundtrack of the storm are burnt into my memory for the rest of my life. And ironically now, at the peak of the storm, as the locals start panicking, I calm down. I analyze the wind speeds, the pressure, the wind direction and I understand the eye has already passed us, it will be over soon. The worst lies behind us. After a short break, when the eye comes closest to us, the pressure stabilizes and the wind kicks in again, strong, yes, but more constant on the storm's backside without those terrible gusts. I know we are on the ramp down, we have made it!

We live!

Epilogue

In the morning, cell service is still gone and power on the island is out. It will take two days until cell service will be operational again. We have a few torn-up headsails, some flipped dinghies, a few fender benders and some coconuts left their marks like big-bore bullet holes on decks and hulls, but no major damages.

The maximum recorded winds on the island were 85 knots, too much for many trees and some roofs. Later I learned that hurricane Delta was downgraded to a category two hurricane just before making landfall at Puerto Morelos, 15 miles south of us, with wind speeds of 96 knots. The minimum pressure in the eye at the time was 953 hPa, on Isla Mujeres the official minimum recorded pressure was 987 hPa.

How good the hurricane hole at Isla Mujeres is, and how lucky we all were, I saw first hand two days later when I visited Cancun. Just five miles away it looked like a war zone, hardly any marina or boat survived on the unprotected shore there. The prestigious marina Hacienda del Mar, for instance, was wiped out.

So, after my first hurricane on a boat, I understand that meticulous preparation, a good hurricane hole, and a great deal of luck are the ingredients for hurricane survival.

The End

Appendix 1:
The Ship

S/V Seefalke is a 40 ft steel ketch built in 1974. She was built by the Dutch boat builder Jachtbouw Noord as Seahawk 37. Her empty net weight is just 9 tons, her bluewater cruising weight almost 12 tons.

With her center cockpit and her high flush deck she sails extremely dry and safely. Hardly any spray makes it into the cockpit. She has a full keel that is flattened on the bottom so that she can easily fall dry in tidal waters. Almost 50% of her net weight is inside the keel giving her extreme stability despite the low draft of just under 5 ft.

She sure is not a racer but a reliable and trustable heavy weather boat. She likes strong winds more than light winds that would hardly move her. She is equipped with a 62 hp diesel engine, 700 Wp solar power and 400 W wind power. Together we have sailed more than 15,000 nautical miles so far.

Seefalke and I are the perfect team. Taken apart from each other, *Seefalke* would just be a piece of worthless scrap metal, and I would be a helpless, pathetic land critter, both of us doomed to drown miserably. But together we merge to a proud and powerful unit. Together we can sail the oceans and see the world. Together we will withstand malicious storms and endless calms. Together we have the courage to overcome our fears and venture out into uncharted waters and foreign lands again and again and again... No woman will divide us, no earthly pleasures will corrupt us. We stand together and, when it will be our turn, we'll go down as one.

It's her who makes the man a captain.

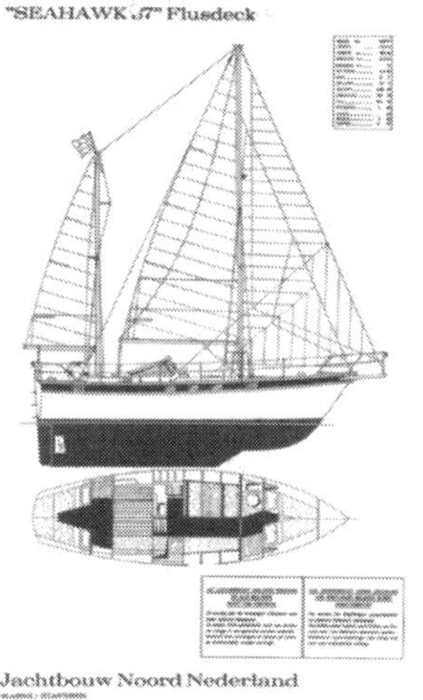

Seahawk 37

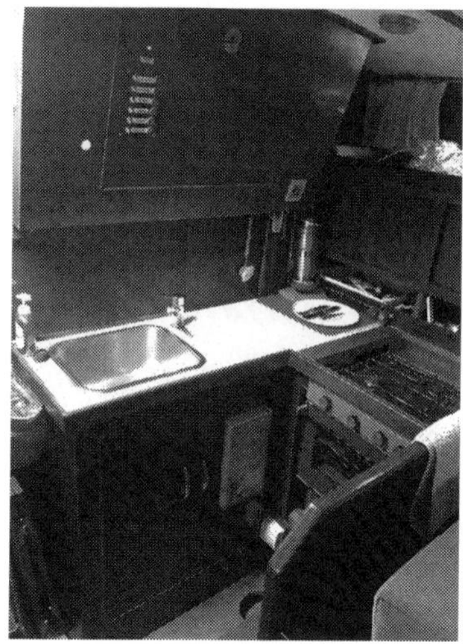

Seefalke's galley

It's the boat that makes the man a captain.
Credit: Lynn Jordan Photography

Solid as a battleship

Boat office

Appendix 2:
The Route

The stories in this book are taking you on a sailing voyage from the equatorial rainforest in Suriname to the Riviera Maya in Mexico.

"Part one: On a Mission" covers the fast pace segment from Domburg, Suriname to Key West, Florida, USA fulfilling my promise to deliver the dogs Cap'n Jack and Scout home.

In "Part two: Culture Clash" I am on home leave in Germany, experiencing irritation and confusion in a world that I had entirely estranged from.

"Part three: Pandemics and Hurricanes" is all about sailing in tough times and vicious waters. It will take us to the infamous waters of the Straits of Florida, the Yucatán Channel and the Gulf of Mexico.

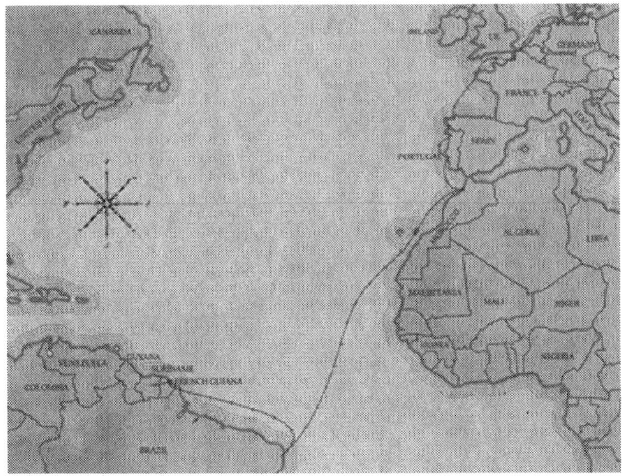

The voyage from Germany to Suriname (not covered in this book)

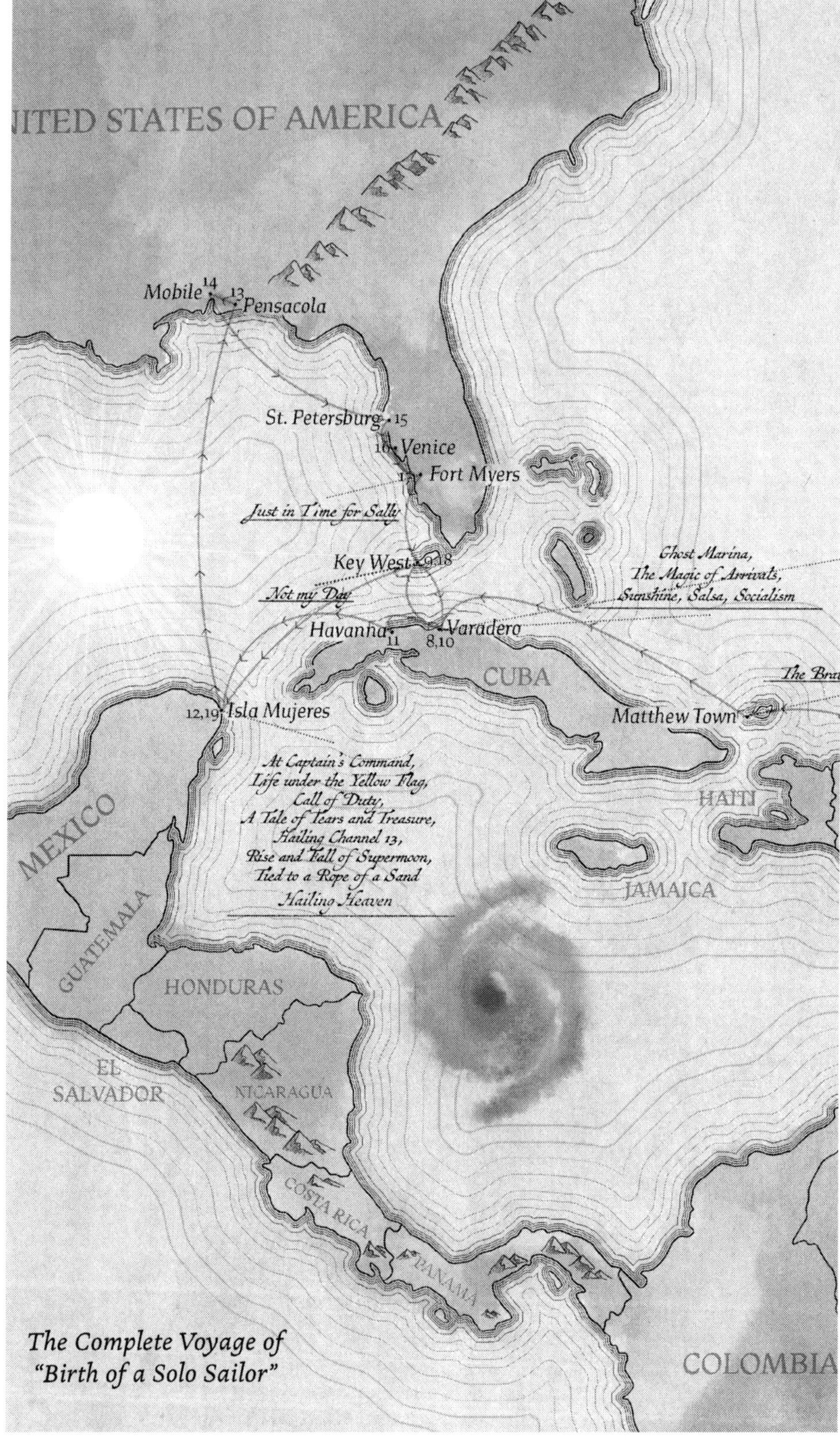

The Complete Voyage of
"Birth of a Solo Sailor"

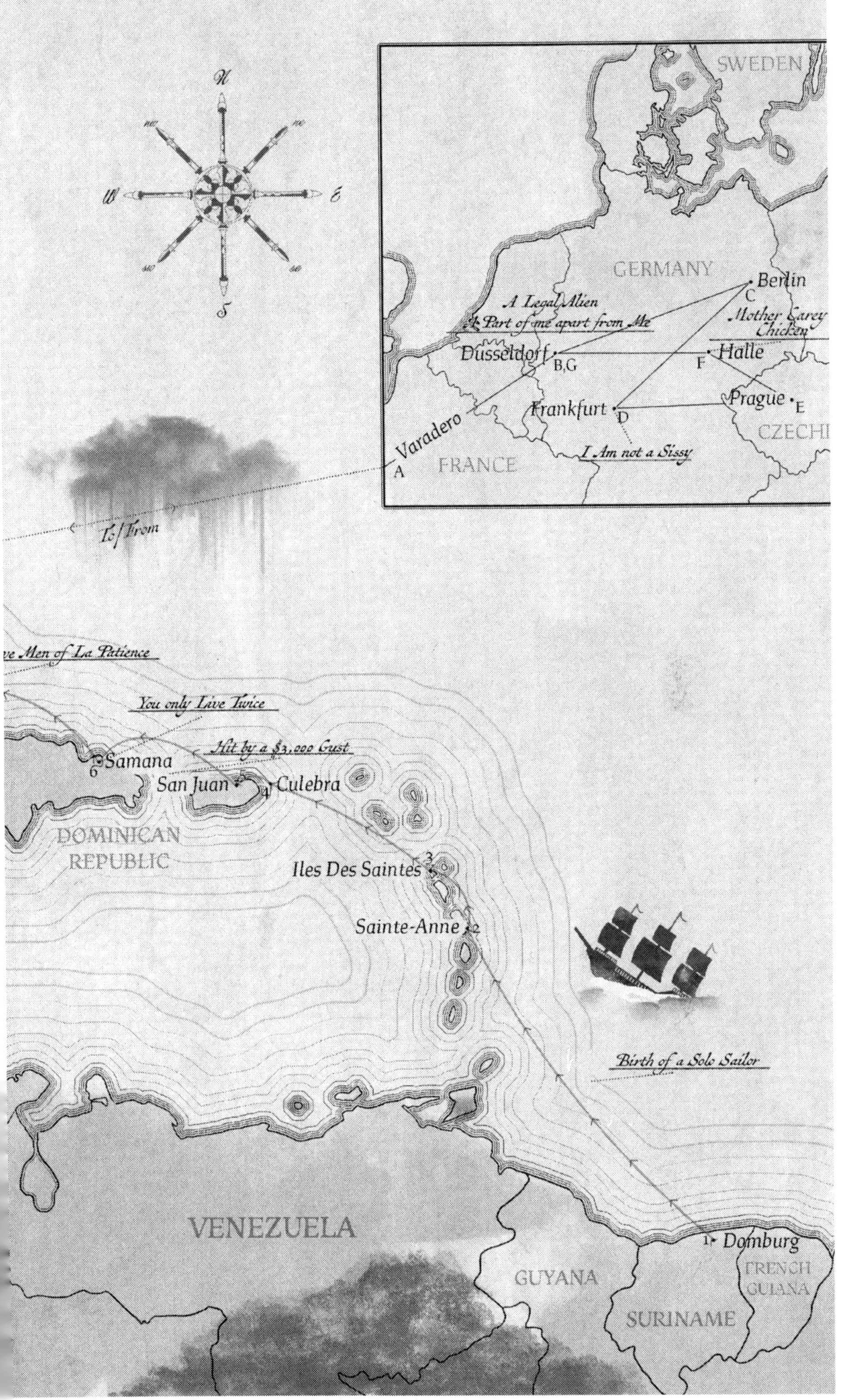

SWEDEN
GERMANY
Berlin
C
A Legal Alien
A Part of me apart from Me
Mother Carey Chicken
Dusseldorf
B,G
F
Halle
Frankfurt
D
Prague
E
Varadero
A
FRANCE
I Am not a Sissy
To/From
ve Men of La Patience
You only Live Twice
Hit by a $3,000 Gust
6 Samana
San Juan
4 Culebra
DOMINICAN
REPUBLIC
Iles Des Saintes 3
Sainte-Anne 2
Birth of a Solo Sailor
VENEZUELA
1 Domburg
GUYANA
FRENCH
GUIANA
SURINAME

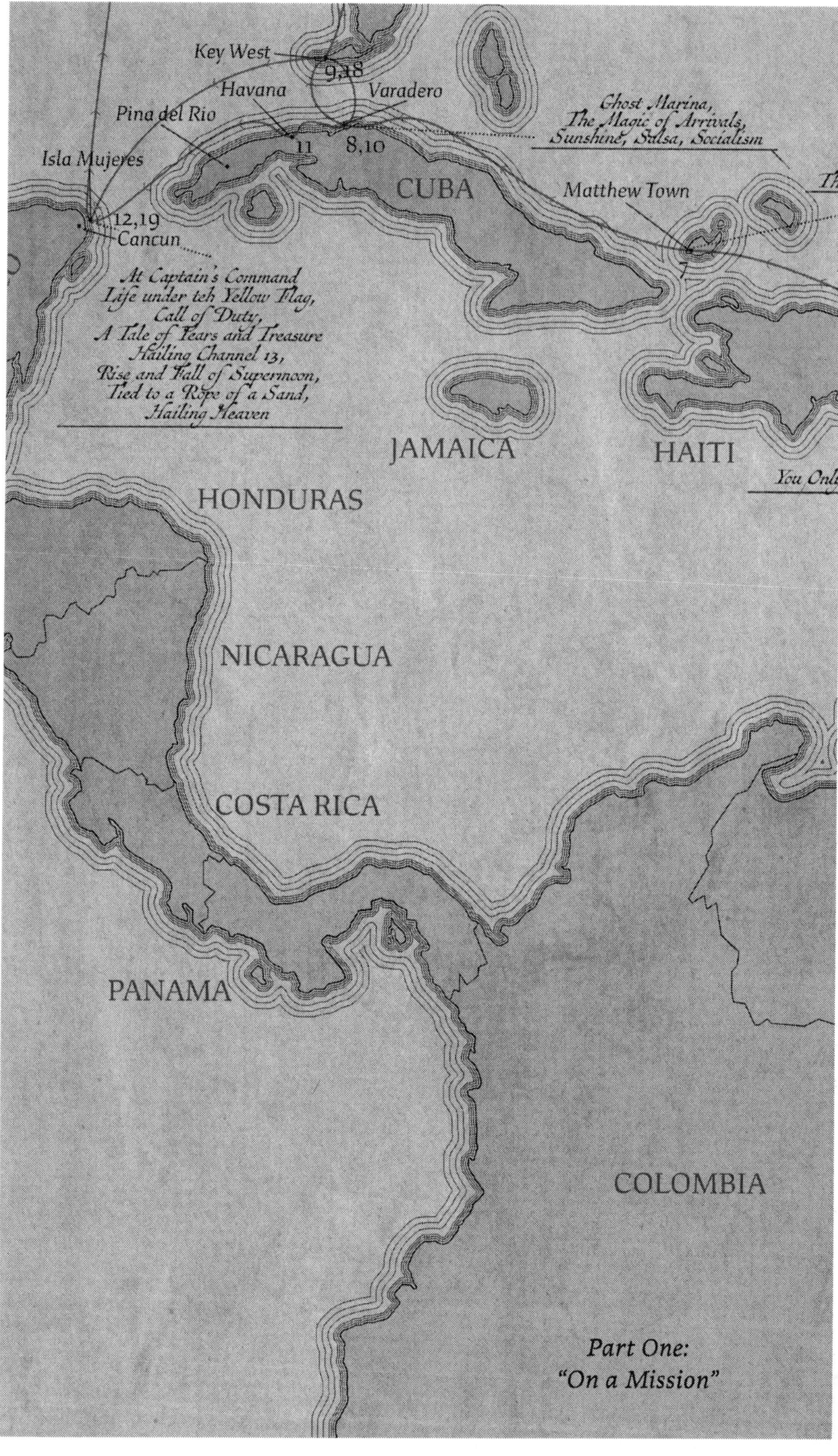

Part One:
"On a Mission"

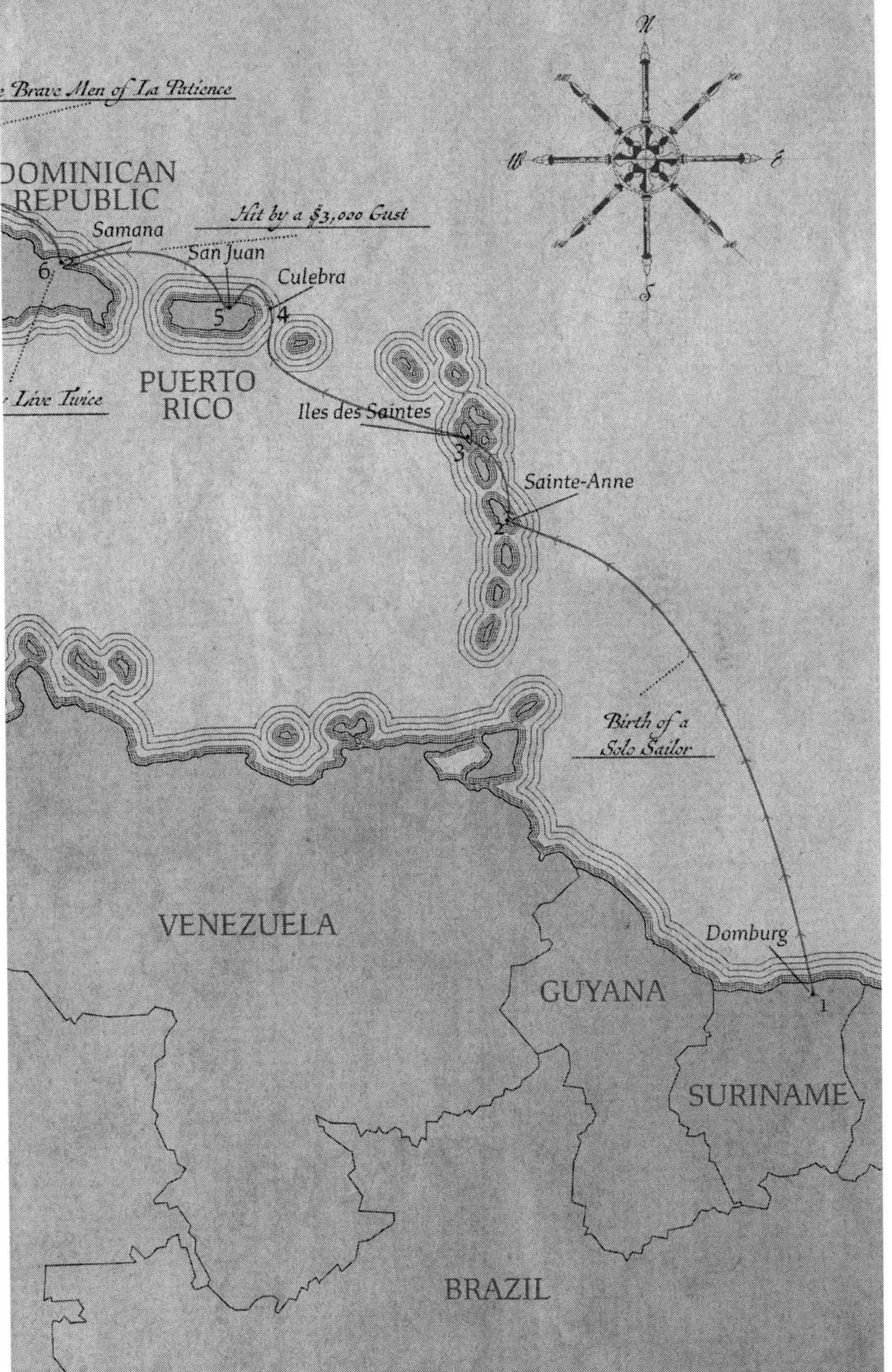

Brave Men of La Patience
DOMINICAN REPUBLIC
Hit by a $3,000 Gust
Samana
San Juan
Culebra
6
5
4
PUERTO RICO
Live Twice
Iles des Saintes
3
Sainte-Anne
2
Birth of a Solo Sailor
VENEZUELA
Domburg
GUYANA
1
SURINAME
BRAZIL
N
E
S
W

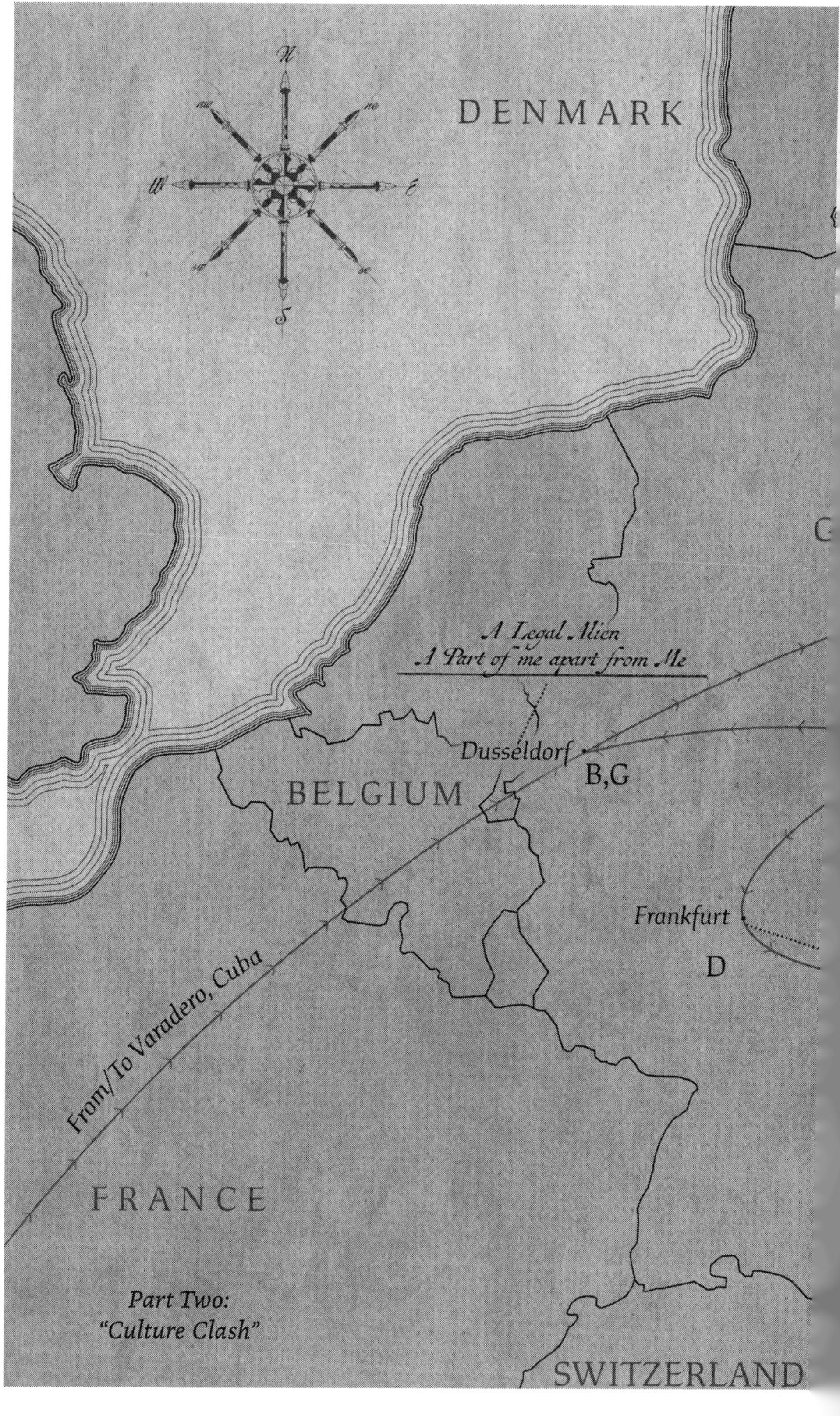
DENMARK
A Legal Alien
A Part of me apart from Me
Dusseldorf
B,G
BELGIUM
Frankfurt
D
From/To Varadero, Cuba
FRANCE
Part Two:
"Culture Clash"
SWITZERLAND

ERMANY
POLAND
C
Berlin
Mother Carey's Chicken
Halle
F
E
Prague
CZECHIA
I Am not a Sissy
AUSTRIA

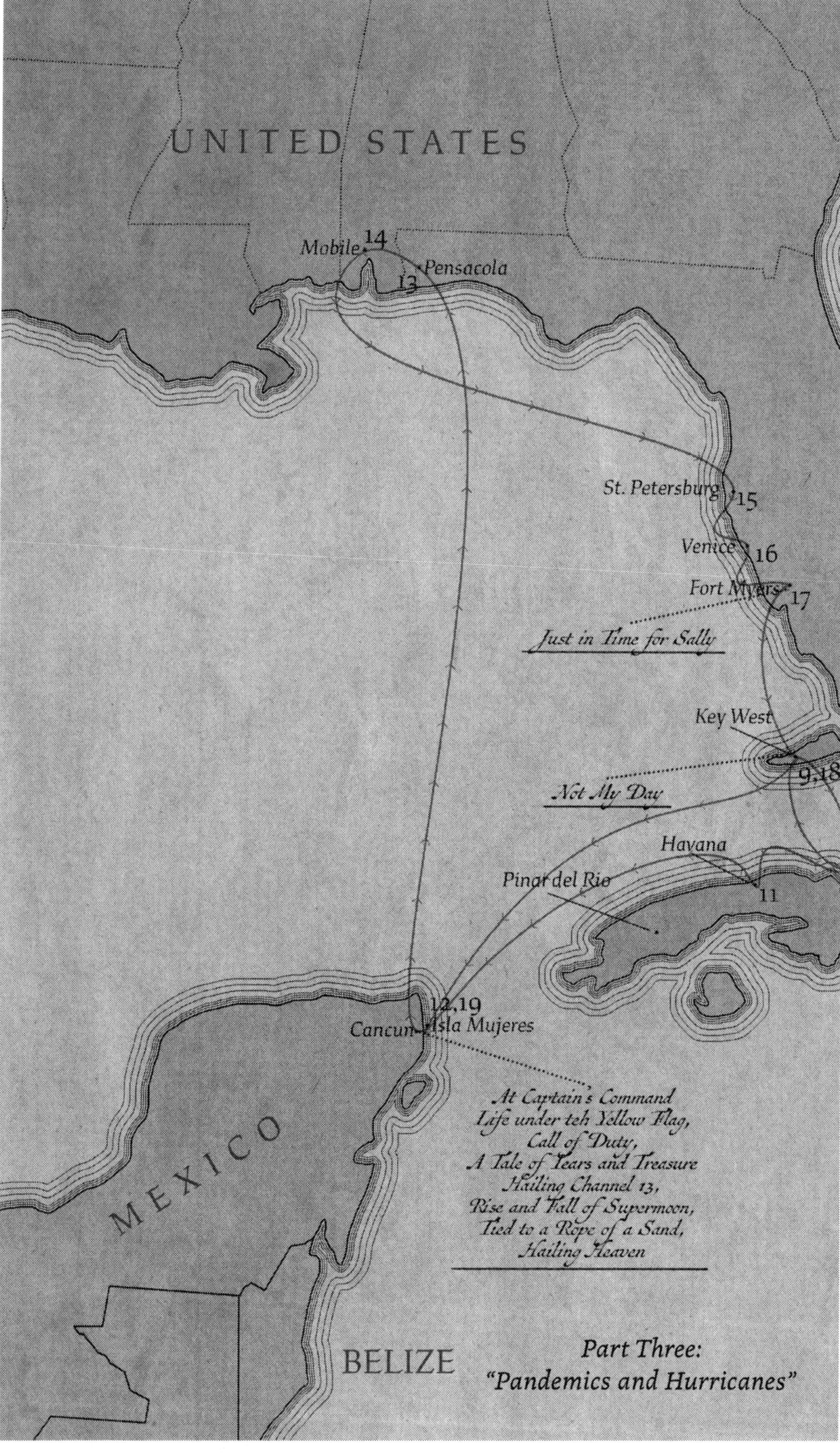
UNITED STATES
Mobile
14
Pensacola
13
St. Petersburg
15
Venice
16
Fort Myers
17
Just in Time for Sally
Key West
9,18
Not My Day
Havana
11
Pinar del Rio
12,19
Cancun
Isla Mujeres
At Captain's Command
Life under teh Yellow Flag,
Call of Duty,
A Tale of Tears and Treasure
Hailing Channel 13,
Rise and Fall of Supermoon,
Tied to a Rope of a Sand,
Hailing Heaven
MEXICO
BELIZE
Part Three:
"Pandemics and Hurricanes"

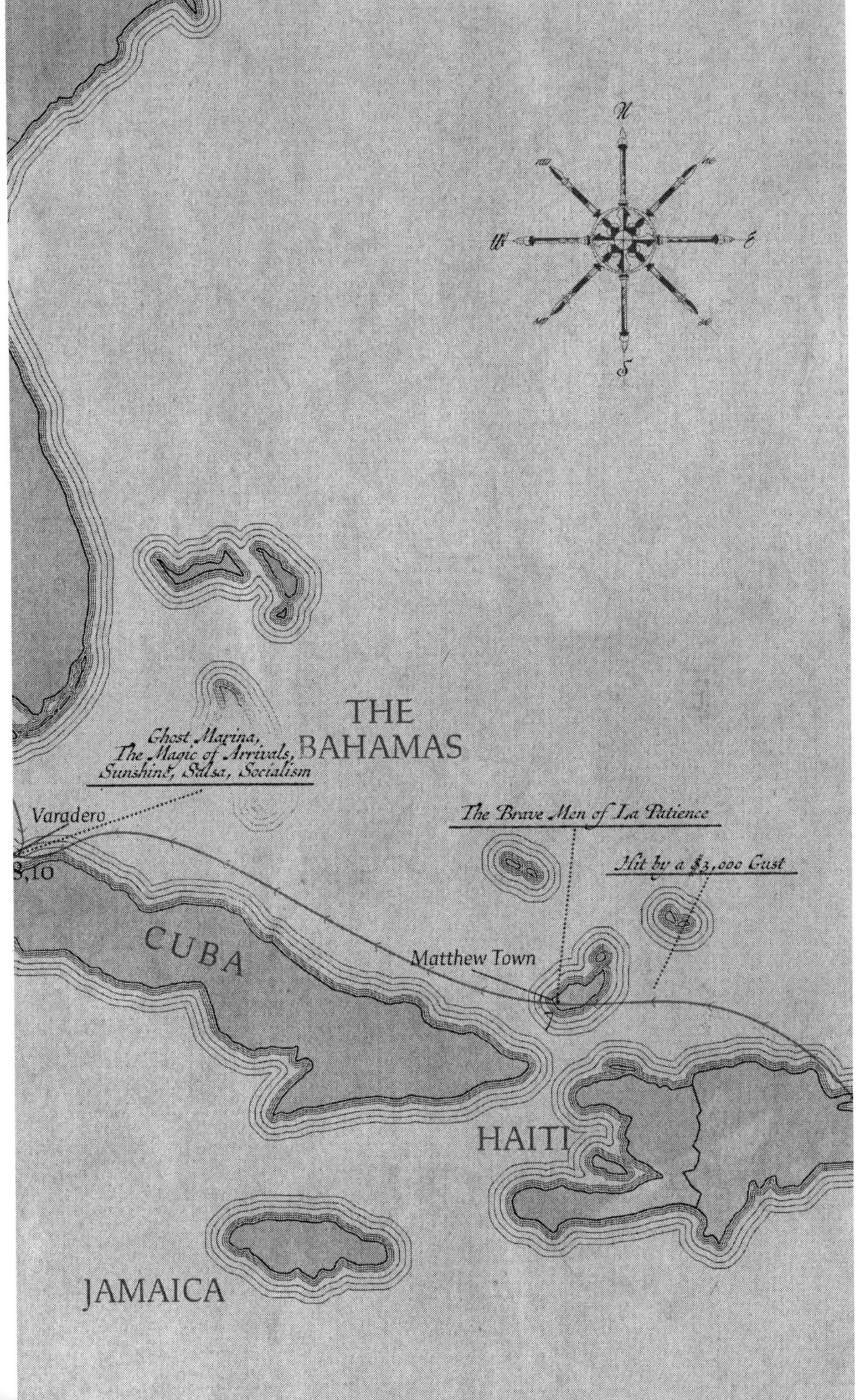
THE
BAHAMAS
Ghost Marina,
The Magic of Arrivals,
Sunshine, Salsa, Socialism
Varadero
8,10
The Brave Men of La Patience
Hit by a $3,000 Gust
CUBA
Matthew Town
HAITI
JAMAICA

Made in the USA
Middletown, DE
03 June 2022